Alexander

DANCING WITH FIRE

Ailish Sinclair

GRAUPIUS

For my readers

1

WHY DOES THE PIANO always echo in a ballet studio? And where does all the dust come from? The floors are cleaned every night. But every day, more dust gets kicked up. I can see it in the rays of weak city sunshine coming through the window. The swish of a foot in a jump, an assemblé, causes white powder to arc through the air. It's a good amalgamation, this one. Lots of travelling across the room and gliding movements too. There's powerful leaps, changes of direction and a wide-armed proud end to the piece. How does it feel to dance it? How would I know?

I'm just part of the furniture here, not even the type of furniture that's made to last. I'm like a garden chair that's been left out all winter to go rusty and someone really needs to throw it away, but somehow I'm still here.

The able-bodied dancers reach the end of class: révérence. Bows and curtseys, oh so polite: thank you, teacher, thank you, pianist, and an aren't-we-great-and-gorgeous glance in the mirror at themselves.

People step over and around me as they exit the studio. No one speaks to me.

I wait for them all to be gone, and then I stand up. I don't bow. I perform a one finger salute to the mirror, and smile. Because that's it. Summer intensive is over. At last. And like I did once in the past, I'm leaving London, and I'm going home to Scotland.

———*ell*———

The door's open. Just a little. Just enough for me to smell chocolate cake and floral soap and wood polish. They're the distinct scents of home, of coming out of the cold and into the warm. I hear singing, and see the soft glow of light from the kitchen.

I stand there in the porch, delaying the moment when I make myself known. I want to extend this between-time, as if the small room, the storage place of boots and jackets, is still some sort of portal to a better life. Maybe I just want a better understanding of all that now. I passed through this part of the house so quickly that first time, all those years ago, pulled along by my excited younger brother. Now, I need to pause. To recall the change, the total transformation of my world that happened when I was eight years old. I know I brought my own messed-up, twisted heart into this house, and though coming here felt like a healing experience, it was a major shock too. It makes no sense, but I want a do-over now. I want to step into the light properly and leave those fucked-up bits of myself far behind. I want so much to—

"Move your arse, birthday boy."

Well that's blown it. Will – stepdad, friend and all round good guy – has just announced our arrival. He's behind me with the bags. My baggage, I guess. I can't carry it because I'm basically disabled. Basically? Nah. Properly. I walk with a crutch at the moment. Like an old man with a cane. However – silver lining – old men are well liked in this house. One in particular. Mine. But enough about him. Everyone knows I'm here now.

Many voices speak at once: "Alexander! Alexander! Alexander!"

The kitchen is filling up with like, literally, everyone. Which means I only get a quick hug from Amalphia – she smells of chocolate cake and home – before I'm engulfed. There's Faye, my little sister, Anna, my even littler sister, Alexei, brother and best friend, and then Bubbles too! The presence of my other best friend is a surprise. We almost became more than friends at the end of last term, but then I went away down south. And, though we texted a lot, we never spoke about it, that 'more than just friends' thing. So I'm not sure it's still a thing. And if it is, maybe it shouldn't be. Because she deserves to be with someone much less fucked up than me.

"How's the ankle?" she asks, looking at me like she's actually asking a lot more. We're careful like that with each other. We don't demand information, but we provide the opportunity to speak it, about some things anyway.

"It's okay," I say, shrugging, not actually wanting to speak about it, any of it, in front of, literally, everyone.

"I'm concerned about how long it's taking to mend," says Amalphia, all dark eyes and hair next to Bubbles's blue and blonde. Both women nod in concern.

"He was just too brave for his own good," says Bubbles, referencing the accident that broke my ankle.

"I know; you should've hopped on the other foot after it happened," adds Alexei. "Dad thinks it was bearing your own and Aiden's weight on the joint, right after you broke it, that's made it worse."

And with that, in he comes. Aleksandr Zolotov, once famous, once great (apparently), once blond, now kinda grey, still tall: and still my father. Not to be confused with Alexander Zolotov, me. 'Alexander with an x' as Alexei used to call me when I first came here. Ten years ago now.

"Alexander," says my father, and he claps me on the back. And that's that. No 'how are you?' and no mention of the fact that he thinks my injury is more or less my own fault.

Bubbles pulls out a seat for me at the long kitchen table, and Amalphia gets me some water so I can pop a pill, because, yeah, my act of heroism in rescuing an idiot from the sea is still 'giving me some gip' as Will says, whatever that means. Hurting, I guess it means hurting. I'm hurting.

More people fill the kitchen. There's Ariel and her husband Jonasz and their three babies. Wow, they've grown, the babies. They can smile now. And they do. They sit on their parents' knees at the table and smile at me. They're not identical triplets, but their smiles all look the same. Ariel tells the babies that I delivered them. Yeah, such a hero. Not. Like I didn't want to turn round and run out of there. Right out of that cave and up onto the hill, but that's another story. The babies look suitably unimpressed with the tale of their birth, even my little namesake, Alexander, called Alex, Alex with an x.

"So, you're coming of age tomorrow," says Sophia. Another little sister, Will's daughter. She was here when I first arrived all those years ago. She's at Uni now, doing clever computery things with her twin, David.

"They're all in a right state about it," whispers David, across the table to me, but in a voice so loud that everybody hears.

"There is no state," states my father. "Just concern."

"About me having my own money?" I say, assuming he's talking about the inheritance I'm getting when I turn eighteen. Tomorrow.

He frowns. "We don't even know if there is much money. The concern lies with..." Wow. It must be bad if he doesn't know what to say.

Amalphia takes over. "We don't want you to read too much into things that shouldn't be focused on. I mean, it may be fine, but we don't know."

That's... confusing.

"There's a big fat letter for you at the solicitor's," explains Will, always the most direct of my parents. He holds up his hand, finger and thumb displaying just how fat a letter he means. Quite fat. Fat like my student file in my father's office. "From Michelle," he adds.

Ah. Oh. Right. I don't know what to think about that. I remember her as a nice, kind grandmotherly person, which is what I thought she was at first, my grandmother. But she was actually my mother. Real Mum, Michelle. And I seem to be pretty much alone in thinking anything 'nice and kind' about her. Everyone else thinks she was a nutcase. Or actually evil; there's been definite hints of evil when she's been mentioned over the years. Which isn't often. Maybe this letter will fill in the gaps. Explain things that... Yeah, of course, things that my father won't want explaining. Like how he had a kid with her when he was with Amalphia? I'm only a couple of years older than Alexei. And I've done the math.

I look right at him, my father, straight into his face, and say: "I'm sure I can deal."

"We don't know what's in the letter," says Amalphia. "It may just be Michelle telling you how much she loved you, because she did. I know that." She lays her hand over her heart when she says this. She's told me before that whatever differences she and Michelle had, they made up at the end. No hard feelings. Not so for my father, I'm betting. Amalphia goes on: "But we know she was unwell sometimes; she struggled with her mental health."

"I get it," I tell her. "It's cool."

I don't think I've comforted her much. Or him. I see her rubbing my father's arm and squeezing his hand. Will joins in, his hand on the shoulder of the great Zolotov. All hands on deck for poor, poor Aleksandr, having fucked-up me as a son.

But then there's Bubbles. Right beside me. Telling me what I've missed at the castle during my extended summer intensive. In the first two weeks of term my father has been a great morning class teacher (apparently) but mainly everything's the same. No Aiden, he's gone back to the States. But there's a new boy. Some twat named Davin. Bubbles obviously likes him. A lot. She smiles when she speaks about him. Which is a lot, both the smiling and the speaking about him. And I don't like it. Not one bit. She gets these stupid instant crushes on people sometimes, and they do her no good. No good at all.

Maybe she picks up on my mood because she goes quiet for a moment and then says, real simple and straight like it means a lot: "I missed you."

"Yeah?" I would like to tell her how great it would have been if she'd been there at the intensive with me, how awesome and funny and cool the summer would have been then, but I don't. Somehow I just don't speak the words.

And when she leaves after dinner, as we stand in the garden, there's an invitation in the air. Like maybe I could go through the woods and back to the castle with her? I want to go with her, and yet, I also don't want to go with her. She feels my hesitation, and I think she misreads it. But I really don't want to fuck up what I have with Bubbles. I mean that literally: fuck up. As in, have sex with her and be a massive disappointment. Have sex with her and ruin our friendship.

So, looking a bit crushed, she heads for the woods on her own. That's the Alexander effect. I have to do something about it. I can't leave her hurting like this.

"If I inherit a million tomorrow, I'll buy you a car!" I yell after her as she makes her way down the darkening garden.

She turns and yells back, hair a golden cloud in the dusk. "I can't drive!"

"I'll teach you! With or without the millions!"

She laughs. And then she runs off into the forest. And I wish I could too. Run with her through the trees, past the pool, into the castle and up the secret stairway to bed. I wish things could just be that simple.

I turn to go back into the house and see that my father has been standing behind me all this time. Watching. Listening. And I wish he wasn't in my life.

2

I'VE SAT HERE IN the stone circle for a long time. Like, a stupid long time, much longer than I sat in the solicitor's office. Much longer than it took to listen to the reading of the will and hear the news that no one was expecting. Even the car journey was far shorter than this, though it was awkward so it felt longer. I didn't share any of the information I was given with Amalphia and my dad. They stayed outside in the waiting room, so I'm still the only one that knows it all. I'm the only one that's wondering: could this be my do-over?

My bum's actually dottled. That's a Holly word, dottled. A word for when you've sat on an ancient stone so long that your bum has taken on the shape of the stone and gone to sleep. Holly is the housekeeper at the castle. The castle, that I'm about to... Nah, am I really?

Yes. I am. It's what I have to do. It's what I want to do. And absolutely no one is going to like it.

I lie down on the stone and stare up at the sky. I do this for a long time too. The puffy clouds change as I look at them; they elongate and stretch out into something smoother and harder looking. All golden on top but dark and red down below. Like me. Golden on the outside, so people say anyway, but dark and messed-up inside. And I need to change, like the clouds have just done. I need to take back what should never have been given away. The red light catches Michelle's letter, or letters as is more accurate – there's lots of them – where they lie beside me on the stone. It looks like the bundle of papers is on fire, but, of course, it's not.

I'm on fire. In a weird kinda way.

I want to text Bubbles and tell her to meet me up here so I can speak to her about everything. She likes the stones. And I can always tell her stuff. I know her dark stuff, and I hope she knows she can tell me more of it if she wants.

But this is different. If I really go through with this – yes, there's still an 'if' – I'm about to make her homeless and school-less. But I can't think about that. If I think about that part too much, I might just chicken out. And carry on with everything being the same as it's been since I arrived here. And I can't do that. I really can't.

I text Will instead. I tell him where I am, and that I could do with someone to speak to.

And then I carry on just lying here. After a while I sit up and watch the shadows stretch across the circle glade like the clouds above. The shadows of the stones are long. They seem like they're pointing towards the castle. The castle that's mine now. Completely mine. Legally mine. It was never owned by the educational trust like everyone thought. It was only in their care. And they're happy to continue on in that manner. Well, they can fuck off. I almost said that in the solicitor's office. But I stopped myself.

I don't stop myself now. "They can fuck off," I say out loud with anger. There's no doubt in my mind anymore. Things have got to change, and I'm going to make it happen. It's time to get rid of all the fucked-up and the messed-up stuff. This is my do-over, and I have to see it through. "They can fuck all the way off," I say about the trust, and my own broken parts, and—

"Hey," says my stepdad, stepping out of the trees. "I hope I'm not included in that?"

ele

The Cottage

Dear Alexander,

Happy Birthday! Congratulations on turning eighteen! I don't need to be there to know what a wonderful young man you are. You're clever, caring, talented and beautiful. I hope you're happy too.

My intention in writing to you is to try and assure that happiness. There have been many drafts of this letter as I decided what to say, and what not to say. What details do you need? Do the details matter at all?

At the time of writing, I have been observing your interactions with Amalphia and her family for some months. You are eight years old, and growing happier and healthier each day. I am at the opposite end of life. I know now that I have months left at most. My biggest fear is that you might make the same mistakes I did, letting people use and abuse you, letting yourself be blown this way and that at the whims of others, becoming marginalised in the process.

Your father is a man who always forces his agenda: don't let him. Strutting about the castle as if he owns it! I hope that can be stopped now. But that is up to you.

Amalphia keeps him in check somewhat, sometimes, but I have no way of knowing if they are still together or whether she has finally seen sense and left him.

I have no doubt that she will still be in touch with you. Her affection for you is very real, her influence entirely benign. I advise you to turn to her when you need advice, Will too; they work well as a team, always did.

So, dear son, dear Alexander, if you take one message from these letters of mine, it is this: take what is yours in this life. Do what you will, make your mark. Have your fun too, for life is about joy as much as anything, or it should be. Our time on earth is fleeting, so make the most of it. Take life by the throat, be true to who you really are, and stuff the others. Your deepest desires and fears often show the way. Don't be afraid to follow them.

The entries that follow were written during our stay together in the cottage. How long we will continue to live here, I don't know. I pass the pages to my solicitor as I write them. I hope you find some sense and understanding from it all.

Live your life, my dear, dear boy. Be happy.

Your mother,
Michelle Manteith

———ele———

I stay hidden away in the room at the top of the tower while it all happens. The changeover. The school moving out of the castle. I can't really believe it's happening. I was kinda expecting someone to find a way to stop it, to stop me. But they didn't.

I know I'm being a coward, a monumentally massive melt in fact, by doing it this way, hiding away instead of facing everyone. But, it's all I can do. I couldn't make my legs carry me out of this room just now even if I wanted to, even if my ankle was fine.

I switch my phone off and lie in the bath of the ensuite. I discover that I can watch the bedroom TV from here, through the mirror. Floating in the water. Mindless. Waiting for one stage of life here at the castle to end. And for another to begin. The door's locked, so no one can gain access. Not to my room, not to me. Noise-cancelling headphones on, I don't even know if anyone tries.

Out of the bath and back in the bedroom, lying on the comfy bed, I look up at the ceiling with the window in it. Through the hexagonal glass, I watch the stars and the clouds and the rain. The sun doesn't show itself for the four days I stay holed up in here. And neither does Amalphia, or him, my father. It's only Will I'm speaking to just now. Only Will I want to see. He might be in the thrall of the great Zolotov, but he doesn't let it affect how he deals with me. He's supporting me. He tells me that. And that's really, really good, because I'm sure no one else is.

I try not to think about how they all must be feeling. What they must be thinking. But I can't help it. Bubbles. Amalphia. Ariel. Though Ariel doesn't stay here at the castle now, and she's still on maternity leave from school. Would that make her the easiest first friend to contact in this new situation? Or are they all ex-friends now? I've thrown them all out of the castle, after all. See, too much thinking. Doesn't help.

Then, end of day four, no sunset, just grey sky above, Will comes up to the room and tells me: they're finished. The school has left the building. Everyone has left the building. So, I'm safe to come out. Not that I wasn't safe; he's keen to make sure I know that. He tries, once more, to tell me that no one is angry. Yeah, right.

But, he's right in one thing: it is time for me to come out of the room, for me to walk through the hallways and rooms of the castle. My castle. Time to see what this change really feels like, and where it can take me. Will I manage to take life by the throat like Michelle advised? We'll see.

3

IT'S QUIET. No, THAT'S not quite right. The building is full of echoes. Echoes and old air. Like it's breathing. Like I'm just one very small component in the history of it. One foot on a black tile, one on white, I look up at the inside of this castle. This castle that I own, I remind myself again. Carved stone angels look down at me from the foyer ceiling. Some blow trumpets. To celebrate my arrival? The return of a Manteith to the castle? Or do the trumpets sound a warning, a dark prophecy; do they blast out a song of doom and destruction? If it's about me, that's fully possible.

The sun comes out, suddenly lighting the huge room, and I laugh off the doom stuff. What bollocks, as Will would say. He didn't stay very long. He's off on another tour in a couple of days, but says I can call him anytime. He's genuinely supportive in his words, but I caught him looking at me as if he's just waiting for me to say it's over. Everything can go back to normal with the castle, and the school, and the students. But it can't. That's over. The angels can blow normal out the door with their trumpets if they like because Alexander is here to stay. Alexander with an x. Me. Me and my keys. I jangle the large ring of them and decide to start exploring.

Places that I know so well look different now. I'm a guy with his own swimming pool. It's all echoey and cold through by the pool which makes it hard to feel happy and excited like I surely should be.

Then there's the theatre. Yeah, well, I won't be using that. That's something else that's over. I'm never going to do another plié or tendu or any of it. Simone, Fake Mum, had me on a hardcore ballet regime from as young as I can remember in an attempt to turn me into something that would impress my father. How messed up is that? Plus: it didn't work. He's never been impressed. So: end of.

I walk up the stone steps to the first floor: step, shuffle, tap; step, shuffle, tap. Yeah, that's not some fancy 'time step.' I'm a broken little boy, not a tap-dancing genius, and that's the sound I make with my crutch in this echoey place. Along the first-floor corridor I go; all the pictures are still there on the wall. I wasn't sure if they would be. What's mine, and what's my father's or the school's anyway? Who knows? Who cares?

They're great spaces, the dance studios, though. And I have money now; Michelle has set me up for life. I could put some sofas in the biggest studio, with a giant TV and some game consoles, all the latest ones, the best games. Lexi would like that. If he's speaking to me. If anyone is. I still haven't checked my phone. Or email. Or anything. It's like I've spent four days rebooting. Four days living on pop tarts and crisps. I wonder what's left in the kitchen?

Sticky notes, that's what's left for me in the kitchen. Holly has stuck them to everything, all yellow and pink and blue against the old white and black and brown of the place. On the great big freezer: *look in here!* There's meals and meals and meals. All Holly's specialties: shepherd's pie, lasagne; there's bought pizzas and ready meals too, and frozen soups and cakes. All with stickers on, cooking instructions.

I wipe my eyes. Must be the cold. The fridge has some of the same sort of notes but with a bit less food in it. All the things I like are there, though. Chocolate puddings and cheese and some veg. There's a post-it on a head of broccoli: *for vitamins*. The old stove has a lengthy explanation spread over several sticky notes on how to use it.

It all sounds a bit complicated, so I'm glad there's a microwave. I use it now to heat up some soup from the fridge. I sit at the really long table. It's like a new version of the one in Amalphia's kitchen. That thought makes me remember something. That old table came from here. By rights, it's mine. As is the four poster bed and the harp, and no doubt a bunch of other stuff he's nicked. But it's okay if Amalphia wants them. It's okay if she keeps them.

I read the twenty or so colourful notes on the table as I dip Holly's homemade bread into the soup and eat. I learn about the heating system, the alarm system, the fuse box, and the lights, both inside and out. There's a really important cupboard somewhere along the passageway that I'll have to have a look at for all of that. And lots of names of tradesman, but the final note is probably right: *or you could just give your cousin a call*.

Good idea. I don't think Ross will mind any of this. And I bet he'd love to help. As long as he understands that Simone is not welcome here. But he'll get that, he'll know, I think.

It cheers me up thinking about Ross. I should have one friend, other than Will, left in the world. I don't want to think about any of the others, but I guess I'll have to face them at some point.

I step, hop, shuffle, tap all the way out of kitchen, down the corridor, across the great hall, under the angels and into the elevator. Thank God for the elevator. It only goes up to the top of the tower or down to the dungeon studio, so it doesn't help much with the other places like the upstairs studios. But, for now in this moment, it's a life-saver.

There's my phone. On the bed. Didn't switch it on for four days, but I've kept it close by and charged. Weird. Oh well. That's me.

There's so many messages. And you know what? I can't deal. Select all. Delete.

I'm shaking as I go into my contacts to do the same, but then I can't do it. I can't just delete them all. I wipe my eyes as I look at all the names. It's only just coming to me how monumentally pissed off they're all gonna be at me, and no, I don't need to hear or read them saying it. But then... there's actually one other person, apart from Ross, on the list who might not be pissed off about any of this at all. Because what I've done doesn't affect her. Like, not at all. And she might be interested and want to chat about it. She might even want to come and stay. And then I wouldn't be alone. So I hit call.

4

AMALPHIA'S HERE. AND SHE'S wearing one of those medieval-style dresses with the lace-up front. She could have stepped straight out of the past, a beautiful ghost, a purple lady come to haunt me in my new abode. She's all big dark eyes and wonder, gazing up at the overhead stone angels, and then she spots me on the stairs and smiles.

"Alexander," she says, her actress's voice filling the huge room, even though she speaks quietly.

Amalphia's entrance always feels like happiness and comfort and protection has just arrived. But it also always feels like I'm not ready for those things, or good enough for them, or even able to cope with them. And today, I really want to know her reaction to what's happened, to what I've done. Seeing her like this makes me realise that maybe this, her reaction, is more important than anyone else's.

I start to make my way over to her, and for a moment, I think she's going to cry, but she squares her shoulders and speaks instead.

"I'm not here to discuss any of it," she says. "Don't think that. I just wanted to see you, and bring you some food..." She proffers a laden picnic basket, the food actually covered with a red-and-white checked cloth, like it's out of a cartoon. "I'm checking that you're okay, basically," she adds.

"I'm okay," I confirm – shuffle, step, tap – finally reaching her and standing right in front of her.

"Good," she says, knowing it's not true as her eyes take a careful scan of my face. "So, can we have a cup of tea and something to eat? Just a mother and son at lunch, no serious talk, nothing scary."

"You're not my mother," I remind her, this feeling very important too.

"But you're my son."

I shake my head, because I want this to be properly acknowledged now. "You've never felt like a mother to me."

She frowns and puts the picnic basket down on the floor, and then there's a clattering on the stairs behind me. Oh no.

"Ally?" calls a sleepy voice from behind me, bringing home just how stupid one of my recent choices may have been. "What you doing down here? It's all dark and creepy and— Oh! Is that Amalphia? I loved her last film."

My new guest at the castle starts to make her way towards Amalphia, but I manage to intercept her halfway across the black-and-white chessboard floor. It's like she's a pawn, and I'm a knight keeping the Queen safe.

"Go back upstairs, Chantal," I hiss at her. "I'll be there in a bit. This is private." My words echo in the tomb of a room, sounding all wrong and fake, like lines from some crap on TV.

"Ally." Chantal puts her hands round the back of my neck and smiles, head tilted to the left. "I just want to meet her; I never got to say sorry when I was here before, and she's a proper, bona fide celeb. Maybe I could get a selfie with her? Pwetty pwease? Oh."

Chantal's hands drop in disappointment, and we both look over to where the picnic basket sits, abandoned, on the cold floor.

It hurts my ankle to run to the door, but I manage. I haul the heavy thing open, but there's no sign of Amalphia on the drive or lawn. My crutch and I tap and step through the labyrinth of dark kitchen corridors, the setting of childhood games, but I don't find her there either, or outside round the back of the castle. I suspect she's hot-footed it up the stone circle path, but whatever, wherever: she's gone. She doesn't want to speak to me anymore, or have lunch. And I still don't really know what she thinks about all this. About me.

Back in the foyer, I lift the cloth off the basket and my favourite homemade chocolate cupcakes with the little silver stars on top stare up at me. Fuck. Fuckity fuck, fuck, fuck.

Questions, questions, head full of questions. What upset her? Me saying she wasn't my mother? Or Chantal being here? Or both? And is that important too?

"Can't you phone and get her back?" demands Chantal. "Even a tiny vid of us together would be great for my channel."

I shake my head. A disturbing thought has occurred: why isn't anyone giving me any grief about anything? Why didn't Amalphia? She must at least be upset about my father being upset – she always is – and he must be, like, really upset, right?

Chantal is full of questions too. "D'you think she'd agree to do a make-up tutorial with me? Share 'tips of the stars' for my followers? Movie make-up? Amalphia's eyes? Because that would be awesome, Ally. Can you imagine how many views I would get?"

"Not gonna happen," I tell her.

"What, you won't even ask?"

"No." The idea is laughable. My old friend and I are using each other just like we did back in first year at the castle, but I'm not going to allow her to exploit Amalphia. Not again.

Chantal tosses her long dark hair, takes her phone out and calls a cab, and then flounces off outside to wait for it.

So, I'm alone. Again. And I don't like it. I stand there, in the hollow-feeling foyer, wondering what to do next.

The castle door opens. Again. She's back. Chantal, that is.

She smiles, apparently having forgiven me. "Meant to tell you, I took some money from your bedside table," she says. "I'm going shopping. You want anything?"

I smile at her; the two of us are still useful to each other. "Yeah, actually. I'll text you a list."

She blows me a kiss and is then properly, if temporarily, gone.

I sigh, and even that feels loud here in the castle.

I sit down on the black-and-white floor. I take off my socks and stretch out my feet, pressing my toes onto the cold stone tiles. My bare skin against the bare floor of the castle. One foot on black. One on white. One good ankle, one bad ankle. Part of me good, part of me bad.

I wonder how long Chantal will be. Hours, probably. She'll have gone to Aberdeen. So, is it worth my going back upstairs for my pain meds, or will I wait for her to arrive with the ones she's gonna buy me? Gonna have to learn to leave stashes in more places; this castle is too big to tap and shuffle back and forth all the time.

And then it happens. The thing that I thought would happen before. And I realise I've really needed it to happen. I've been waiting for it, and it's such a relief. The world makes sense again. Well, some sense.

The big Gothic arch of the front door bursts open in a flash of blue skies and sunlight and a man is silhouetted there, his fury clear from his stance, though his face is in shadow.

"You arrogant little twerp," says my uncle Justin, not the person I expected, then stepping inside. "You really think you can get away with absolutely bloody anything, don't you?" he says as the door bangs shut behind him.

I shrug. I have gotten away with it. I mean, it was legally left to me. "I can do whatever I want with my own castle," I tell him.

"Your castle? Your castle?" His voice rises in pitch with every word.

I get up off the floor. I stand up to face him. It seems wise. I've just remembered something else that I've disrupted. The major televised event that was planned for this term. The major family event, in fact.

"Is this about your wedding?" I ask.

"My wedding?"

"Well, it was going to be here—"

"I'm not talking about my wedding, boyo," says Justin. "Or 'your' castle. I'm talking about Amalphia and how you treated her this morning. Telling her she's not your mother? What sort of thing was that to say to her?"

"But she's not my mother. We're not related in any way." Why do people never seem to understand this?

Justin's mouth drops open, and his cheeks redden as if he's shocked and furious all at once. "When has she ever let that matter? Tell me: has she loved you any less than the others or treated you any differently because of it?"

I just look at him. Because I don't know the answer to this question about love. How can we know about the affection that someone else feels? Or doesn't feel, for that matter. Is there a way? I don't know. Maybe it's the big question of my life? Does Amalphia love me? Does anyone?

"You hurt her so much," my uncle goes on.

Did I? Really? And, if I did, what would that mean? I'm not ready to go there yet, so I just say: "I very much doubt that."

And Justin punches me in stomach.

5

So, I'M HOLDING A box of chocolates and standing in the porch of my house now, well not my house, I guess my house is the castle now. Weird thought. True thought.

"Go on, then," says Justin from behind me. "Go in."

But I can't. I have to knock. Now. I knock quietly on the upper part of the stable-style door.

"Oh, for pity's sake," my uncle says and pushes past me and into the kitchen.

I follow him in and discover that the kitchen is full of everyone that I don't want to see, everyone that I'm not ready to see.

My father blocks them. For once his presence provides minor respite. He stands in front of me and holds out his hand, and then he shakes my hand as if he doesn't know what else to do. Then he holds my one hand in both his.

Okay, this is way too weird. I can't look at him. I'd rather have the abuse that must be about to come from the others. I pull my hand back, step round him and look at them, my friends.

Ariel. Bubbles. Henry.

They don't look angry. Not exactly. They look questioning. And I'm suddenly struck with the feeling that I can't believe what I've done. Did I really claim the castle as my own and kick everyone out? Am I really that big of a jerk?

Speaking to my friends is delayed anyway as Justin starts up with his story about how punching me in the stomach was like punching a wooden board or, "A washboard, if you will," as he says. "I'm lucky my hand's only sprained," he tells everyone. "This is your fault, Phi. You fed him way too much protein over the years, and his muscles have got no give in them at all. We spent the whole afternoon in A&E."

There's a chorus of demands for explanation, and my uncle is in his element explaining how he hit me while 'defending Phi's honour,' which is unfortunate wording.

My father looks me straight in the eye. "I knew there was something I was not told. What has heppen?" Decades in the UK, you'd think the accent would be less.

Amalphia says it was all a misunderstanding, and then she springs into her ordering-us-all-about thing that she does. My dad is sent to cook stuff, Justin is told not to hit people, and everyone is reminded that this is to be a nice dinner: family time, no arguments. My friends are told they can have me later; she needs to talk to me first. I'm pushed back into the utility room. I guess that means I really am an adult now, if I'm being admitted to the grown-up, secret-talking place of the house.

"I am so sorry," she says, and that's all wrong, but she holds up a hand, halting my disagreement. "We all made assumptions about you and how you felt, especially me, I think."

She's searching my face for the truth of this. I shake my head like an idiot.

"But tonight's not the time for deep talking," she goes on. "We're all here. Together. And that's important. Whatever's going on, there will always be a place for you here; this is your home."

Now she's hoping I agree, so I nod, and she smiles.

"I'm actually a little bit whiffy," she says and frowns. "No, I don't mean whiffy; I hope I'm not whiffy." She opens the door to the kitchen and announces: "I've had a little too much wine, and I'm squiffy!"

I step into the room behind Amalphia, and they hug me. All three. Ariel. Bubbles. Henry. I want to cry. Like a total loser. But I manage not to.

"So are you like me now?" asks Henry. "Speaking-wise?"

I laugh. He's not wrong. Henry used to only say one word at a time when I first met him. I haven't said a word since I came into the house.

"So, how's it going in the castle?" Ariel asks me. "Now you've thrown us all out? Are we banned from the premises? Will we be shot on sight if we approach the door?"

"No," I say at once, seeing what I hope is a sparkle of laughter in her eyes. "You can visit any time. It was just, you know, something I had to do."

She nods in answer to my inadequate explanation, and her phone buzzes. "Jonasz," she says, looking at the phone and frowning. "I need to call him."

Which leaves just Bubbles to speak. She smiles at me, and it means a lot, and I so wish I'd called her. I wish I'd talked to her about all this.

"Henry and me are staying at Ariel's," she tells me like it's a normal sort of news, and with no hint of bitterness as to the why of it. "We're coming here to do classes in the upstairs studio; do you know about that? Sorry, I didn't mean to..."

"Make things awkward?" I fill in for her, and we both laugh. And then I remember something. Something from part of Michelle's jumble of letters. And I have to do something really fucked up to her, to Bubbles.

"You know that necklace I gave you last year, the mermaid locket?" I say to her. She nods. "I'm sorry," – I really am – "but I have to ask for it back now." I don't really have to, but I really want to. I want to see it. I need to study it.

"Oh," she says. I guess I make all my friends frown now.

And then she only goes and pulls the locket out from under her pink fluffy top and hands it to me. She was wearing it. I think about that as I trace the pattern of red rubies on the surface of the gold disc with my fingers. What does it mean, that she was wearing it? Did she do that because I was going to be here? Or does she wear it all the time? And if so... No. I can't believe that.

But I don't have time to do more than thank her and pocket the thing because food is ready, and we are all ordered to the table. There's quite a crowd tonight, with Justin's partner Kian being here too, and his son. The youngest children of the family are absent, I notice, along with Will who's off on his tour now.

As we sit down to dinner at the huge table, it's increasingly obvious that Amalphia is definitely what she said: squiffy. I've never seen it before. She's always been so together, running round after us all; this is new, and... I don't know what to make of it.

My father takes it in his stride, buttering a roll for her as she slops soup onto the table while trying to dish up. But then, he's happy because he's getting all her attention; she rubs his thigh, kisses his cheek and gazes at him in a soppy way. It's always been a two-pronged sword this, though they're generally more discreet in front of us all than they're being tonight.

On the one hand, I get it: their unusual relationship. I'm totally cool with the whole polyamory thing. But I don't like seeing her being affectionate to him, my father. So I adjust my vision. I blur my eyes. I've been doing this since I was a kid. I know it's weird, but it's always been sort of comforting. It's easy enough not to look at him too closely, and then he becomes me and her love is being directed at me and not him. And when I was younger, it felt awesome because it was like I got to be loved, to believe that I was lovable... and he didn't; he wasn't. But I'm not a little kid anymore, and I know it's super-weird, and super-inappropriate. It's super-secret too, of course, and I guess it shows how completely fucked in the head I really am. I stopped it last year, but here I am again, falling straight back into my old twisted ways of trying to feel better.

"Oh. You're here." It's Lexi. His appearance in the room shakes me out of the super-weird. "I thought you didn't want anything to do with us anymore?" he says to me.

I'll have to speak to him. Later. Explain. I really didn't want to upset him, and I really don't want to lose him, the first person who ever looked at me like he liked me, loved me even, if you don't count Michelle, and I'm not sure if I can, count her, that is...

"Alexei," admonishes Amalphia.

"Let him get it oot," advises Holly, the second motherly presence in this family, the formidable matron of the castle.

In ousting dear old Dad and my friends from their school, I have done her out of a job, and I'm more than a little worried about whether she's furious, or 'fizzing' as she would say.

"It's all very well keeping quiet and being nice," she continues, "but big things hiv happened. Ye canna just wash it away like pudding out of bedsheets."

"It's not like that," I try to tell my brother, who's obviously seriously pissed at me. "It wasn't planned. It was just something I had to do."

"Right," he says as he takes his place at the table, but he doesn't sound convinced.

There's a bit of a silence after that until Amalphia hiccups and giggles and drinks more wine. Her husband's arm rests on the back of her chair, his thumb brushing up and down the back of her neck. She moves against it, like a willowy tree in the wind, all natural and—

"Oh, Alexander," she suddenly says, head jerking up in my direction. "You didn't bring Chantal." The whole table is instantly interested "I didn't mean to be rude to her," Amalphia explains. "She'd be welcome to take a selfie with me."

"Chantal? Chantal who was expelled in the first year? She is at the castle?" That's my father asking the incredulous questions. But they're all over everyone else's faces too, those questions.

Ariel's eyebrows are high, Henry looks astonished, but the worst is Bubbles. She looks like she's been punched in the stomach, like I actually was earlier. But harder. Like lasting damage has been done to her. And I'm sure she thinks I wanted the necklace for Chantal. Which is total bollocks, and how could she think that? For a moment, I'm angry. Which is really dickish of me, considering. Because Bubbles's thoughts make sense given the context. I have a weird moment where I suddenly wish I could undo everything I've done recently. Take it all back. Because I've hurt Bubbles. And that seems worse than anything. But if I undo everything, then everything will stay the same, exactly the same, including me, and that's no good for any of us.

My parents are still talking about Chantal, and I realise I'd forgotten all about her. As soon as Justin appeared today, Chantal exited my mind completely. She'll probably have arrived back to the locked-up castle and gone home, gone away and left me to stay there alone again.

"She's gone," I say. "Chantal's gone." I mean, it's probably true.

Probably. The word makes me think of the historical TV show Bubbles and I did together last year, and all the 'it is thought' and 'probably' stuff that got tagged onto 'facts.' We laughed about that back then, the two of us. But we're not laughing now. She's not even looking me at all anymore. And I think she's the one who's gone now. She's the one who matters, and the one I've lost. Forever. Probably.

6

"It's not a bad idea to have some company there, Alexander," my stepmother says from across the table, looking straight into my eyes. "And I'm sure Chantal has matured since we last saw her."

It's good of her not to mention that Chantal was expelled from the castle for stealing some of Amalphia's own underwear and putting it up for sale online. We all know it anyway, of course. And I'm not really sure she has matured since then. Which shows how stupid it was of me to invite her up here. I didn't think of that at the time. I was just stressed out being all alone and too much of a coward to contact anyone else.

Amalphia continues: "The castle feels bad. D'you remember the creepy feel there was when we were first there?" she asks Justin, who nods. "And then it got a bit better when there were more of us. Well now..." She pauses, her cheekbones looking more defined, hollowed out somehow. "It's as if all the bustle of students and music and laughter was keeping it all at bay. The coldness, the silence; it's like it's let evil in from below, allowed it entry again—"

"Hello!" sounds a call from the porch.

The stable door swings open, revealing an extremely thin woman and allowing a gust of cold wind to scatter small yellow leaves across the floor. Summer's really over.

"It's only me." says Fake Mum, Simone, as if expecting delight or relief or some sort of positive reaction to her presence. Talk about evil being allowed entry.

"No," says Amalphia at once. "Not here. Never here. This is Alexander's home and—"

"It's okay," I say, surprising myself for a second. "Let her stay."

Everyone is shocked. Bubbles and Ariel are asking if I'm sure about this. Amalphia's eyes have never been bigger. My father's frown has never been more pronounced. He's really uncomfortable, and it's almost worth letting Simone stay for this alone. But the truth is that I want to see her. Now. In the entirely changed circumstances. Michelle left me everything. Simone got nothing. And I want to look into her eyes. And see what's there. And see what I feel about it – her, everything – now.

"It's okay," I repeat, Simone not having moved from beside the door, as shocked as all the others, I think. "Sit down opposite me," I suggest, pointing at the empty chair.

"Well, how lovely," says my sister, my half-sister, and she takes me up on the offer at once. "I guess you do remember all that I did for you."

"Oh, I remember everything." I say the words slowly, emphasis on 'everything.'

She twitches as I glare right into her eyes, and I enjoy it. Her gaze flickers away from me, and I smile.

"Have some soup," I say, and the large tureen and a bowl get passed down the table, the very silent table. All eyes are on Simone. And me.

"Is it low fat?" asks Simone, recovering herself, or pretending to.

"No," barks my father.

"Oh, well," she says. "I'll just have a little."

I study her. If my staring is making her uneasy, all the better. There's no sign of it, though. She's ladling soup into her bowl, and plenty of it. Some people look great with really short orange hair. Simone isn't one of them. It has to be her stupidest makeover yet.

"I had to come, you see," she says, looking round the table, at everyone but me. "It's not every day your only son turns twenty-one!"

I look straight back at her and laugh. "I'm eighteen. This is not my birthday, and I'm not your son."

"Ha!" shouts Amalphia, thrusting her wine glass into the air. The dark liquid spirals upwards and lands in a line across the white tablecloth, splattering Justin quite badly. Tiny specks hit my face, and we both laugh, Amalphia and I, united in humour for a few seconds.

"Phi!" complains Justin. "Time for the main course, I think, Aleks. Curry, isn't it? Give her some rice to soak it up."

"Let her be," my father tells him. "When does this woman ever let loose and relax? When does she unwind?"

"Aye, it's long overdue," agrees Holly from the other end of table.

"Unwind in a different direction next time," urges Justin. "The young ones have less expensive clothes."

My father refills his wife's glass and fires off directions, and the twins and Lexi cover the table in dishes. There's three different curries; two types of rice, and naan breads aplenty.

He helps his wife to it all, and I really look at her. I look at Amalphia. She's kinda deflated; she's watching him with the usual adoration, but there's a limpness about her I don't like. Did I do that to her with what happened earlier? Or is it because Simone's here?

"I've seen Amalphia drunk before, of course," Simone tells us now. "On what was actually the most magical night of my life."

"Oh, stuff it up your arse, Simone." Amalphia. Being flat out rude to Simone. I love it.

"Ha!" my father agrees, lifting his glass high, and Justin ducks to avoid more escaped wine.

"Are you squiffy too?" Amalphia asks him, holding his face, studying it.

"I am," he says.

"We're behaving badly." She giggles.

"So, this is what happens when your little girls are not here, is it?" asks Kian, Justin's partner, just recently in remission from cancer.

"Not usually," Amalphia says, deeply serious. "But you make a good point, Kian; the younger children are away at a sleepover, so we're all adults here. We should do something mad! After dinner, let's all dance naked in the stone circle!"

Keaton, Kian's son, a bit older than me, splutters wine across a tablecloth that may be completely beyond salvation now, much like the battered old table beneath it.

"We were conceived there, in the circle," says David. He's random like that. A bit like Will himself. He's not here tonight, Will, still being away on his tour. Which is a shame. He would have said a few choice things to Simone, I bet.

"I'm sensing people are not up for nudity," reflects Amalphia. "So how about ballet? Upstairs. Aleks can teach us. It's been ages since I've taken class."

"And you think tonight, in your current state, is the best time to recommence?" Justin pauses in thought. "As performance art, though, it might be fun. Just you two; we'll watch."

Amalphia gives Aleks a strange look, and then suggests a food fight.

"Now, this is an Amalphia I can get on board with," announces Keaton, and I want to hit him.

He's always so disapproving about stuff; if he's not looking down his nose at Amalphia's cakes, he's running a finger along windowsills searching for dust. Why Lexi bothers with him, I don't know.

"Keaton," warns Kian.

"No, no, this is good," says Amalphia, swigging back more wine and giving Keaton her full attention. "I want to know," she tells him. "You liked me when you were a little boy, running about playing zombie games, but then it changed. What went wrong? How could I have been better, made you feel more welcome here?"

"No, that's just it," says Keaton. "You're too welcoming. It was always: 'Are you warm enough? Have you got enough to eat/wear/read/watch? Will, take Keaton with you; see if Keaton wants this; is Keaton all right up there in his room?'"

"That is enough," says my father.

"Too fucking right, it's enough," I say, agreeing with the old man for once as I look at Keaton. "Have you any idea what it's like to be brought up in a house where nobody gives a shit? To be left alone all night, hear shouting and banging at the door and wonder if you're going to be killed? And then know, absolutely know, that no one would give a fuck if you were?"

And I realise that this is really why I dislike Keaton. What right does he have to be dissatisfied when I had it so bad and he had it so good? He was here, for fuck's sake. Sometimes, anyway. However, I've silenced the table, the room, the house. I can't quite believe I said all that out loud. I can't bear the look on her face, Amalphia's face, and try to put it right. "Coming here was like walking into a new life," I tell her. "Onto another planet. It was heaven."

"Dude," says Keaton. "I just meant she needs to chill. And she is tonight. And that's good."

"It's very hard being a single parent," points out Simone, an oft-spoken mantra from my childhood. Poor, poor Simone, burdened with having to look after and attempt to perfect me: disgusting, unlovable me.

"It's time for you to leave, Simone," Amalphia tells her, her voice loud and firm. And cold, so totally cold.

"Wha-?" gasps Simone, hand flying to her neck in shock. "But I haven't—"

"Yes, you need to go," says Bubbles, and I look at her in shock. Her voice is a growl and her face is so angry she almost looks like a different person.

I didn't mean to upset Bubbles and Amalphia like this. I turn to Simone and look directly into her empty, soulless eyes. "Leave," I say.

She raises her chin as she looks back at me, defiant, I think.

"You heard him," says Amalphia. "Out. Now."

I've never heard Amalphia be so cold, or so authoritative. She has spoken in a way that can only be obeyed, and Simone scrapes her chair back, stands and walks out without saying anything, though there is a short display of loud sniffing as she passes through the porch.

Amalphia smiles. "There could be something to this over-welcoming issue; I need to work on it. Thank you, Keaton."

"Yeah, no, Amalphia," he stutters. "I didn't mean any big thing. You've always been great. Really. I think I've had too much to drink too. Not that you, I mean..." He turns to Lexi. "Weren't you going to show me that guitar?" And with that, the two of them leave the room, Lexi not having spoken one word during the meal.

"Faye could do with her own room now," muses Amalphia, as she watches the boys leave. "Anna could have Keaton's room. I mean, he's hardly ever here... Sleeping bag on Alexei's floor from now on, I think. No, actually I can't do that to him—" and she stops, suddenly in the place I was not minutes before.

Amalphia's parents didn't love her either, and I just know that's what's in her mind at this moment.

My father holds her, and she leans her head on his shoulder, eyes full of sadness.

"That boy grew up thinking his mother didn't want him," she says, and I'm confused. Does she mean me?

"Well, she didn't," snaps Justin.

"He shouldn't have known it so young, though," says Kian, letting me know they're talking about Keaton. "Or, ever, really. And that's on me."

"Parenthood is difficult," says my father, and there's no doubt that he's talking about me. "It can be very hard to know the right thing to do or say."

I turn my head to look right at him, and his frown deepens as his eyes meet mine.

"Aye," declares Holly. "Noo. I brought pudding. Whisky-chocolate mousse. Who's up for it?"

Ariel is not up for it, not just because of the whisky – she never touches alcohol – but because she's texted to check in on her babies, and Alex with an x won't stop crying.

So they're going: Ariel, Bubbles and Henry. I walk out with them, wanting to say something to Bubbles, but not knowing what, so I end up saying nothing at all like an idiot.

Ariel gets into the car and says: "Come and visit soon, Alexander. And maybe, you know, actually speak to us." That's good; she sounds happier than before.

Bubbles looks at me before she gets into the back of the car. But it's not good. It's not happy. It feels like more of the 'gone from me forever' thing I sensed earlier, and I turn away from her and walk back into the dinner party.

7

BACK IN THE HOUSE, everything feels different. There's still plenty of people left, but the place feels a lot emptier somehow. I sit down at the table by my bowl of chocolate mousse.

The twins take their pudding off upstairs to eat while working, though Sophia checks first: "Mum, are you sure you're okay?"

"Yes, darling, absolutely," Amalphia tells her. "I had brandy by the fire with Kian and then wine through here with Papa; you know I don't usually drink, so it's gone straight to my head." She puts her hand on my father's chest, as if to say, 'He's here with me, I'm fine.' But she's not fine; he can't go back in time and give her a nurturing childhood; he wasn't there for hers, and he wasn't there for mine.

She's focused in on the pudding, making that noise she makes for cake, turning to him, involving him in her sensuous swirl of chocolate and sex. "We love chocolate mousse," she tells everyone. "Thank you so much for bringing it, Holly."

"Aye," says Holly, eyeing the two of them with suspicion.

Amalphia sucks some stray mousse off her finger with an accompanying sound that's almost a snarl and my father tips his wine into his lap.

"Oh dear, you'll have to get changed," she says, all wide-eyed and fake innocent.

"Yes, I think this also." He nods, so serious.

35

"There's some clean trousers in the ironing cupboard," she tells him. "I'll come and help you find them."

And with that, they're gone, Amalphia taking a bowl of chocolate mousse with her.

"Aye," says Holly again. "Well, some things niver change. They always were a pair o' randy buggers for each other."

"No way," exclaims Kian. "Not in the middle of dinner, with people in the house?"

"I hate to say it of my dearest bestie," drawls Justin, "but she is very readily up for it, or has been since she met the Zolotov."

"The way I see it," says Holly. "It was always Phi 'n Aleks... Hold on." She gets up and shuts the door to the hall after peering down it. "It's nae the same with William; that's more of a spiritual connection."

"I would have to disagree," says Justin. "They're the worst. Public places, desks, offices..."

We all look at him in surprise.

"Emotzia," he says, naming the contemporary dance company that Will still runs, some of time anyway. "They've been walked in on there a couple of times, in the office; then there's the balcony in London, oh not actual sex, but serious inappropriateness. They once stayed in bed for two weeks; that was before, between, after all the business with Kelly..."

"What exactly happened there?" I blurt, because I've always wanted to know, and never felt able to ask.

They all look at me as if they'd forgotten I was there.

"Well, you're eighteen now, I suppose it's okay," decides Justin and then fixes me with his hard stare, usually reserved for underperforming TV assistants. "You've seen Phi lose it a little bit today; oh, she perked up as soon as you came through the door, but earlier you and I both saw her fall apart. Happens to her when she thinks she's lost someone she loves. She absolutely can't cope with that. Happened in London; when she thought

36

she'd lost Aleks, and again when she realised she still loved him: major meltdown. It was ugly, but when Phi and Hearst made up, it didn't matter who was around."

"Aye, yer right enough there," concedes Holly. "I was forgetting the stone circle."

"Yeah," says Kian. "If you don't know where those two are, you're not gonna walk up there."

Justin sighs fondly. "Still, it's healthy, isn't it? And it's working. They've been married, coming on for twenty years now, so they must be doing something right. Let's see if we can get them to admit that the secret to a good marriage is lots of sex. When they come back through; that'll be fun."

They make coffee and open the chocolates that I brought, which were actually meant as a sorry for Amalphia, but it isn't long before she appears and takes one.

"Phi," says Justin. "We were just remarking on the length of your marriage – crap, now I'd rather equate it with the length of something else – but no, no, tell us. What is the secret to a long and happy marriage?"

"Love," she says with a smile.

Justin shakes his head. "Too clichéd, too vague; specifics please."

"Chocolate," she says. "Oh. Wait a minute. What's happening about your marriage, your wedding?" Her glance darts between me and Justin and Kian.

"It's all sorted," Justin tells her at once. "It's still going to be in the castle in two weeks' time. No problems."

"Oh, thank you, Alexander," she says and gifts me an enormous smile. "There'll be some things to arrange, insurances and licences that will alter with the new ownership, but I'll see to it, don't worry."

"Phi, you're dodging the question," says Justin, who I now realise did exactly that with my question about the past. "Come on," he continues. "What aspect of the Zolotov has made it so easy to stay married to him all these years?"

Amalphia smiles. "His absolutely enormous... heart."

—ele—

The Cottage

Dear Alexander,

They came here today, Aleks and Amalphia. You were at school. Simone let them in while I, the orchestrator of it all, watched from above.

You've seen my observation screens here in the cottage; you know some of the set up. I hope it won't shock you to learn more of it, though I suppose my way of working is shocking to most people. But it's what I do, you see. My work. My ground-breaking work. Amalphia knows how powerful that work is, though she may deny it. Aleks is clueless as to the import of what he was involved in.

In fact, Aleks is entirely lacking in the ability to see what he has, to recognise the enormous gifts that the universe has showered down upon him. His wife, a phenomenally successful actress, an exquisitely beautiful woman, held his hand today and comforted him. She had just learned that he had a child with somebody else, and this is her reaction. I cannot say I understand it, but I see her strength, and her true worth.

He lost his temper at one point; it was totally delicious. I delighted in seeing him so befuddled about how this woman that he never slept with – Simone – can have had a child who is so plainly his! However, I could see that he caused Amalphia some distress in his anger, but she pulled it all together and invited you to visit their house.

You have every right to go, of course. That house was built by our family but unfortunately sold away some decades ago. It is good that you are to be there sometimes now. There is a rightness and balance in that. There is much for you to learn about our family, about your property. Take my necklace – it should have been given to you. Trace the pattern made by the red stones. It's a map, darling, a map! It shows all the underground places of your world.

But that is where we are, my dear Alexander, at what I hope is the start of you becoming part of Amalphia's family. I hope it has been a happy place for you to grow up. I hope you are appreciated for the beautiful man I know you have become.

Goodnight, Alexander – sleep well.

8

MAYBE THEY SHOULD JUST build a new castle for the wedding. It might be easier. Everything here is wrong, apparently.

Justin is here every day, loudly explaining all the many details of the wrong. "Who designed these stairs? The great hall isn't big enough! Who decided to call it great? It's hardly Westminster Abbey, is it? Well, I suppose the theatre will just have to do..."

But the castle is full of people again, and it's kind of a relief. Though a bit annoying too. And annoying is the only feeling that I let anyone see.

Chantal is still staying here, and I can tell that she enjoys all the extra company too. I suspect she'd have left by now without it. She talks to and films everyone for her channel: decorators, cleaners, caterers, florists, lighting experts, musicians... I know she's been talking about how amazing it is that she's here at the castle, on those videos. You know, after having been thrown out in her first year; now the people who threw her out have been thrown out. And while I quite like the idea of her rubbing that in the face of the man who expelled her, he's the least likely person to watch her channel anyway. My friends, however... But there's nothing I can do about that just now.

Today the marquee suppliers are dealing with a massive erection on the front lawn; Justin's enjoying mentioning that. A lot. It's bigger and more impressive than any erection they've dealt with before. He tells us all that at least three times. Which is a bit funny, I suppose.

The preparations for the wedding are being filmed for a show about Justin and Kian getting married. In a pink castle. But the focus is not just on the preparations. Cameras are following me around a disturbing amount of the time too. I've been labelled the 'bad boy of ballet' which is a bit lame, like me I suppose, given that I'm still hobbling about and also that I'm not famous or anything.

"But you are, Alexander," insists Justin when I point out how stupid it all is. "You are famous. From the competition in your first year, from the historical documentary in the second, and now, in what would have been your third year of school, for kicking all the staff and students out of their premises!"

Chantal walks past us and heads up the stairs.

Justin gives me a meaningful look. "Don't forget you're suddenly rich, darling, and how people always love that."

Yeah, I suppose there is something about me to love now.

ell

It's one of the cameramen who tells me about Ariel. That she's here at the castle. And crying. His tone suggests maybe I broke her heart or something.

I find her in the foyer, baby Alex with an x on her hip.

"Hey," I say, leaning my crutch against the wall and putting my arms round them both.

They seem little and alone and lost in the great big space which really doesn't make sense. Ariel has been here so much, it's like her home. But Alex has never been here before. And today... I can tell that something's really wrong with Ariel. Like *really* wrong.

I take them up to the first floor where the cameras don't get to go, to my new purple sofas and gaming space in the largest of the studios there. There's brand new blankets, fleecy ones, which is good, because we can sit on a sofa while Alex lies on the floor on a soft, fluffy blanket that I fold up just for him. I'm listing things in my head, more things I need to buy for the place. A box of kids' toys would be good. A box of tissues too.

If I wasn't such a slowcoach with my ankle, I'd nip down and get Ariel a cup of tea and something chocolatey, but I think she needs to talk more than anything. And I'm right.

"You know how he hasn't been developing as fast as the girls?" she says of Alex. "But everyone kept saying it was okay and normal?"

I nod. She has mentioned that.

"Well, it's not normal," she tells me now. "There's a hole in his heart."

"No," I say, looking at him. "But he's so great."

"Yes," she says, face soaked and red from crying. "He is great. But he's ill. He's not been feeding as well as the others. I knew that from the beginning. I've been saying that all along, but people just thought I was a stupid first-time mum, so what did I know? He's not gained weight like his sisters."

"So, is there medicine he can take?" I ask, already thinking: stupid question, how could medicine close a hole in the heart?

But: "Yes, he's getting medicine, and extra-rich feed stuff, but if the hole has not closed by the time he's one year old, he'll have to have surgery." And she's in floods again.

"He'll be okay," I say, hugging her to me while the baby gazes up at the ceiling of the studio, unaware of anything wrong inside him. "Made of tough stuff is Alex with an x." I get down on the floor with him. "Aren't you, mate?" I hold out my hand for him to see, and he grabs it, real fast, and real hard. "He is, Ariel. He's strong."

"He likes you," she says as Alex smiles so broadly that I think he might even be laughing. I'm not sure if that's something babies can do at this stage, and I'm not gonna ask in case it's something developmental that might be another issue.

"Maybe he just finds me funny," I say.

"Well, we all find you funny," she says and I'm glad that she's smiling. "So tell me yours."

"Mine?"

"Umm, yeah. Your stuff. Your major stuff. Expelling us all? Living here all on your lonesome?"

"Just something I had to do, Ariel," I tell her. "It feels like a do-over. I didn't want to hurt any of you, but the castle is mine. Not my father's. And he shouldn't have it anymore."

She's nodding, like she knew my feelings about my father were behind everything. I'm not sure it's that simple, but I'm not really ready to analyse my feelings deeply, let alone speak about them.

"You know we're getting to finish our third year?" she tells me. "Bubbles and Henry are staying at mine and travelling over to your dad's house every day, but the others are actually staying there, at your house, Clinton and Paul and Paula and Star and Belinda and Davin. First and second years have been transferred elsewhere, to other schools across the country."

Some of this is news to me, students staying at the house anyway. They weren't there at the weekend. "Must be crammed," I say.

She nods. "But they'll all be going on tour soon. Amalphia and me are going to be teaching in the village hall for a bit, then it'll just be me. She's giving it up."

"Because of this? Because of me?" That's not good. Not good at all.

But: "Nope. She's been thinking about it for a while. But what's a girl gotta do to get some hot chocolate in this place?

Tell me you've got some? And I've got to heat up a bottle of special feed for Alex."

She goes in search of heat and chocolate while the two Alexanders lie on the floor and gaze at the ceiling. It's calm. Nice. Sun shines in on us, and I slide the blanket carefully over so the baby is not dazzled. And then we just lie there again. Just two guys chilling. Hanging out. Two Alexanders with an x.

Ariel comes back into the studio with Chantal. They recognised each other off TV and the internet.

Chantal is actually being really sweet to Ariel, which is a relief, because she can be a bit of a bully if she doesn't like someone. She loves the baby too, and finds it funny that he and I get on so well together.

Alex has his feed and his medicine and goes to sleep on the floor. Then the two girls leave me in charge of the baby while they go through to the next studio where Justin's TV people have set up a professional make-up station. Chantal intends to give Ariel a makeover, no doubt to be filmed for her channel.

Little Alex looks so peaceful. I tuck the blanket round him in case he gets cold, and then drink my hot chocolate in the watery sunlight.

Ariel's hair is in a long mermaid plait with colourful ribbons when they come back through.

I wait till they're gone; Ariel and Alex head home to Jonasz, and Chantal goes off to see what's happening downstairs, and then the older Alexander with an x has his medicine, his painkillers. And he goes to sleep on the floor too.

9

PINK AND COVERED WITH flowers. That seems to be the theme of the wedding that's happening here today. Well, that and the fact it's all being filmed. There's cameras and sound equipment and lighting stuff everywhere, much more than there were with the other TV programmes they made here. The flowers really smell. It's like the castle has become some sort of botanical garden or perfume bottle, inside and out.

"It's a gay wedding in a pink castle," Justin said yesterday when I mentioned my thoughts to him. "What more of a theme do you need?"

However, Justin is not here today, this morning, not yet. He slept at the house. Kian slept here in a lower tower room. To be traditional or something.

And now, Lexi, Keaton and me are standing with Kian and the minister on the stage in the dark theatre of the castle, awaiting the arrival of Justin and the wedding party. They're going to walk down the aisle here, through the audience and up onto the stage.

I smile out at my classmates in the auditorium, none of whom look like they're bearing me any resentment. Except maybe Bubbles. She's not looking my way, not smiling back like most of the others. Clinton waves, distracting me from my study of Bubbles.

Ariel beams at me, little Alex on her knee, the girl babies on Jonasz's lap. He thanked me earlier, for looking after her when she came here. He said it gets a bit much with the three babies sometimes.

Chantal has somehow got herself sat in the front row where she's looking around at everyone. I know she's wondering which celebrities she can persuade to do selfies and videos with her.

And celebrities, there are, Crispin Truelove being the most famous of them. But there's others too. Well known faces. Well known dancers. People that know Justin and Kian and Amalphia and Will and my dad.

Kian's nervous. He's all twitchy as he stands here on the stage.

"It'll be alright, Dad," Keaton assures him.

"Yeah, he won't stand you up," Lexi adds, and Kian nods but doesn't look convinced.

But Lexi's in a better mood, and I'm glad about that. Earlier, he asked me if we could party it up here at the castle after the wedding, and I said yes. So I think we'll be okay now, him and me. I hope so, anyway.

We all relax a bit when Will comes through the door at the back and gives us a double thumbs-up. The wedding party has arrived, and here they come!

Little Anna, the youngest Hearst-Zolotov family member, walks up the aisle first, scattering rose petals in front of her, closely followed by Sophia and David. Next is Amalphia, glamorous in a sleek black dress, flanked by her two husbands, and then Justin arrives arm-in-arm with his mum and Faye.

And we get going. And it's much like any other wedding, really, I think. Until we get to that bit about anyone knowing of any lawful impediment to the proceedings.

"Not anymore," whispers Justin.

"Wait!" says a voice from behind us. "Yes!"

We all turn. 'Gobsmacked' is an Ariel word, and I think it now as I look out at everyone. Gobsmacked is what they all are. It's what this whole room, theatre, is.

There's this older dude standing there. In the middle of the audience. Among the guests. "Well, not lawful," he says, pushing along past people to stand in the aisle. "But, I just had to tell you, Justin, before you do this..." There's a pause. "I love you."

Justin stares back at the man. My uncle is the most expressionless I've ever seen him. Kian is open mouthed, and obviously horrified. This day has been quite stressful for him so far.

The guy continues with his interruption of the service: "I was stupid. In the past. I didn't see the beauty of what we had until it was gone and too late. If you would delay, this, here today, to think about what you really want. I am in love with you, Justin. I always have been. I should never have let you go."

Justin looks at the man, smiles, shrugs, and turns back to the minister. "Go on," he says.

So they do.

There's rings. There's kisses. And there's huge applause.

We make our way up the aisle and out of the theatre, Chantal somehow attaching herself to me and stepping into the wedding party.

"Oh my God, Phi!" Justin whispers so loudly that probably most of everyone hears him. "Edward! Can you believe it?"

"I know!" Amalphia whispers back.

"I hope the sound people caught every word of it," says Justin, ever the producer. "Bit of added drama, you know. I've told them to watch you for the rest of the day too," he adds, turning to me. "Sweet little ballet boy, gone bad. Who's not going to love that?"

Me, that's who. My face hurts from the extremity of the scowl. When was I ever 'little and sweet?' When I was eight years old? And that was— But Amalphia shushes Justin, and on we go.

———*ele*———

Photos of the wedding party get taken everywhere: by the castle door, on the castle steps and the stone staircase, and in a studio. There's ones of all of us, and also of small groups of people: family groups, couples, that sort of thing. The stars of the show get solo pics taken too.

Finally Justin and Kian go to have their own 'boudoir' pictures done in a room that Amalphia has arranged for them. I helped set that up with her earlier in the week. It's one of the bedrooms in the tower, and it's full of flowers too.

The rest of us gather in the great hall, along with the other guests.

There's pink champagne. It combines with the pain-killing capsule I just took in the bathroom to create a really fuzzy buzz. Everything slows and becomes calmer.

I see chocolates. Waiting staff are passing them out. I eat chocolates. Lavender and rose creams. Pink and purple on the inside, little sugar flowers on the outside. Like the castle today, all flowers, everywhere, but you can eat these ones.

I'm on my own in a great big crowd. Like a little lost fish splashing about in an ocean of bigger fish who all know each other. These fish, these people, haven't kicked their friends and family out of the family pool or castle lately, so they're different from me, separate from me.

I see Chantal across the room and start to head towards her, so as to not be alone in the crowd. Then I see that she's talking to Aiden, Crispin's son, who studied here at the castle last year and is the reason I broke my ankle. I didn't know he was going to be here. I should probably mind or care that Chantal's speaking to him and looking so cosy with him. But I don't. I don't seem to have that in me, to mind, that is. My head is still fuzzy.

"You look lost."

Yeah? I always am. I turn to find Bubbles looking up at me. The mermaid of this ocean. She's all pink and pretty and sweet. Kinda like the rose cream that's melting in my mouth. Not that she's melting in my mouth. Stop. Swallow. Speak. Say something to Bubbles.

"You look pretty," I say and realise it's a totally lame thing to have said. Lame, like me in all the ways. Like one of Ross's old horses that had to be put down. But that wouldn't be the right thing to say either and what I said was almost true, but there's more to it, so I say it: "You're more than pretty," I tell her. "You're beautiful."

"Uh-huh," she says. "How many of those have you had?"

I look where she's looking. At the pink champagne. In my hand. "Just this one," I say.

"Look at you, Alexander," she says, doing the up and down, full checking-out thing. "You've grown over the summer, you know; you've got that sexy, long-legged ballet dancer thing going on, more than ever now."

Her words do something to me. They give me a different kind of buzz. A better one. But only for a second, because it's not true, what Bubbles said. I shake my head. "I'm not, though, am I? I'm not a dancer. I sat at the side of all the classes, all summer long. No one spoke to me."

"That sounds shit," she says, like she gets it, but then she adds: "Your eyes are all weird. What have you taken to make your pupils look so big?"

It's confusing. I don't have pupils. I don't teach. That would be Amalphia. That would be Ariel.

"It's not this," she says, tapping my glass. "So are you on drugs?"

Oh. Yes. "Painkillers," I tell her. "My ankle still really—"

"Oh look, it's Bubble-icious!" says Chantal, arriving at my side and taking my arm. "Still sticking to Alexander like chewing gum." She laughs. No one else joins in with her. "Wow, you have not changed, Bubbles," she continues. "Still doing those big cow eyes at my boyfriend." And she does really exaggerated jazz hands. Chantal. It's Chantal that does that, those jazz hands. Bubbles used to do them when she was uncomfortable or unhappy and hiding it. My brain still feels slow, but I get that Chantal is making fun of Bubbles and not in any sort of friendly or gently teasing way. She's being genuinely nasty.

"Nope," I say, really loudly – other people look round. "You're not doing that to Bubbles. You can fuck right off, Chantal. Right out of the castle. And I'm not your boyfriend."

She starts up some sort of squealing angry reply.

I tell her to just leave.

And she shrieks some more. Says no amount of money is worth this.

Many cameras point in our direction, their lenses reflecting the pink of the everywhere-flowers.

And Ross is suddenly here. Right in my face. "Fuck's sake, Alexander," he says. "It's Simone I'm supposed to stop from making a scene today, not you."

"Simone's here?" I ask, incredulous and angry all at once. "In my castle? She was invited to the wedding?"

"I think you've got a family thing to go to," says Bubbles quietly at my side, hand on my arm, bringing me back down to somewhere less twisted than I was heading.

She's right. Justin and Kian are just coming into the great hall. Their photo session must be finished. Amalphia and Will and everyone else seem to be gathering together with them, with the grooms. I struggle to remember what's next on the wedding itinerary, mind still full of: "Simone shouldn't be here. She must have invited herself, like at the house. I won't be saying it's okay this time "

"Leave Simone to me," says Bubbles. "I'll tell her some things and see if I can get her to leave. Eat something solid, Alexander, like a sandwich or a cake, before you go up to the circle."

Oh yeah. There's going to be a blessing thing. In the stone circle.

I head over to the family. Bubbles heads to Simone. And together, I think we've got this.

10

I EAT A SANDWICH. Bubbles was right. Food was a good idea. I feel a bit less fuzzy, and I eat another sandwich, and then a third one too. There's plenty time because of all the intense discussion that's taking place in the extended family group around me. My head's not quite as slow anymore, but I don't understand what's going on.

Lexi fills me in on the drama, the fact that both grooms' dads are here, and no one knows which is which.

"But surely they know?" I say, so glad that my brother and I are speaking normally again. "Justin and Kian at least?"

"Nope," says Alexei. "They haven't seen them since they were little. I'm not sure Kian's ever met his."

"But their mums must know," I point out.

The two mums are standing a little way away from the others with Holly; it looks like they're actually being comforted by Holly.

"Everyone's too scared to ask them," Lexi explains. "They were both determined that the dads were going to come to the wedding, but they're upset now they're here. So we don't want to upset them any more, see?"

I do see. I take another sandwich and then nearly choke on it when someone pokes me really hard on the arse from behind.

"Pass one down here," says a bossy old lady in a wheelchair. She's wielding a walking stick, and I recognise her. She's Amalphia's old teacher, Madame. "Come on, boy," she demands. "I haven't got all day!"

Hasn't she? Haven't we actually all got the whole day today? I hold the plate out and down to her, though.

"Well, aren't you your father's double," she says without taking a sandwich. She's wearing a stupidly big hat. It must be hard to see out from under it.

"No," I tell her. "I'm nothing like him."

"Similar personality too," she snaps back, and I withdraw the heavy sandwich plate and put it back on the table.

But the family group, the wedding party, is moving, and, oh yeah, I'm part of that. Across the hall we go, past the kitchen, out the door and up to the stones.

I guess it's quite cool, the tying of the coloured ribbons round the wrists, and the personally spoken vows of love. They look more relaxed and happy, Justin and Kian, during the hand-fasting than they did at the more formal wedding earlier. They look close and genuinely loving as they gaze at each other. If Chantal was up here, she'd be taking photos and tagging them **#RelationshipGoals** or something.

Kian still looks tired, though. His cancer is in remission, which I'm so glad about, but I realise it makes it even more dickish of me to have forgotten about their wedding when I threw everyone out of the castle.

My parents look like they're enjoying the ceremony. No, not my parents, I remind myself. I only have one biological parent here. Him. He looks particularly pleased with himself, standing between Amalphia and Will, today. I glance quickly round at everyone else here in the circle of stones, checking that Simone has not managed to intrude on this as well. She hasn't. So, it is just the one unfortunate biological relative of mine that's here. But that's one too many.

Once it's over, after the photographer and TV people take many shots and angles of wrists and ribbons, we all move to head back to the castle, and Amalphia comes over to me.

My stomach tightens. My smile widens. The day seems sunnier. I like being up here with her, among her stones; it's just a shame there's so many others here too. I see my father watching us like she needs protection from me or something.

"Do you know which of the dads is which?" she whispers to me. "Justin and Kian's dads?"

It's disappointing that I don't know, that I can't solve this problem for her. I put forward the suggestion that one of them has a slightly naughtier look than the other, so maybe he's Justin's father?

"Wait a minute. I know," she says and calls out: "Justin's dad!"

Both men look round.

She tries again. "Kian's dad!"

They both smile. In the end she takes their arms and walks down the forest path to the castle with them, chatting animatedly and attentively as only she can in an awkward moment.

As we emerge from the trees and reach the lawn, the crowd that's gathered there cheers. Justin and Kian hold up their tied hands and everyone applauds too. The big screen in front of the castle wall is telling them to do that in big bold letters.

Small old-fashioned signs have been hammered into the grass to indicate where 'peasants' and 'nobility' are to go. Nobility gets to be inside for the wedding and for all the foody stuff. There's some buffet-style deal being set up in the flowery tent, the 'massive erection,' for the peasants, the people who are only here for the reception.

But – get me – I'm castle-owning nobility today, and I head inside with the rest of my family.

11

TABLES ARE OUT AND ready in the great hall, and we all take our seats. Amalphia's in charge: she sits the mystery dads together at one end of the long family table near me. I feel her hands on my shoulders and her breath in my ear as she tells me that she's failed in her investigative quest, and to let her know if I manage to work out which dad is which.

She uses a microphone to tell everyone to make their own pizzas as an appetiser – the speeches will be later – and we all tuck in. I know she was in charge of the catering and feel a bit excited about what's to come.

I can only imagine what this is costing per head; in fact, I can't imagine. A fortune, is all. The mini pizzas are keeping warm over a clay/candle set up while the toppings are over ice. I could eat this and nothing else for the rest of my life.

Papa Zolotov soon ruins it all by standing up to give what can only be an insincere monologue about how Justin's always been there for them, during good times and bad, and how he would never be without him and Kian. I've actually seen Justin call my father on his shit a few times, but his toast to the bridesmaids praises Amalphia and Faye to the sky which is good.

Crispin Truelove shouts from one of the round tables in the room: "Hear, hear!"

Amalphia gets the mike again and says, "I've a bone to pick with you, Truelove. Stay put after lunch so I can find you."

"For you, my dearest Honeybee, anything," he booms out, and everyone laughs and claps.

There's a choice of three soups including homemade tomato soup, freshly prepared Scots dishes of *Cock-a-Leekie* (I hear Justin ordering that one, demanding a large portion so it becomes 'massive cock-a-leekie') and *Cullen Skink*.

I choose the tomato, and catch Amalphia smiling at me. Was the dish included for me? I've always loved it. She's always given it to me when I'm ill or upset. Does she think I'm ill or upset now? Maybe I am. Maybe I always am.

Will stands up as the soup plates are cleared by the waiting staff. Amalphia hands him the mike.

"Yeah, so," he says. "It's been a day of guys standing up and saying how much they love Bevan." Someone wolf whistles from the back of the room. "I'm doing something a bit different," Will continues. "If you'd all turn and look at the screen," – he indicates the wall on the right – "I'm going to do a history lesson. Yeah, that's the castle," he says pressing the clicker in his hand as an old photo of the building fills the large screen. I remember the picture from the TV show in our first year here. "It's really old," Will continues. "And there's Bevan when he wasn't quite as old."

A picture of a cute baby appears, closely followed by one of baby Kian. "They didn't know each other then," says Will. "A state of affairs that was just never quite right. Some strange stuff happened." We're treated to the sight of Justin dressed as a banana and Kian in his stripper mode. Man, he has a lot of tatts. Maybe I should get one. I'm eighteen now, so I can. As more bizarre costumes from shows shoot by, it seems weird that I haven't been inked yet. I mean Will has them, Amalphia too. Zolotov doesn't. Plan made.

Amalphia stands and says: "Oi!"

I splutter with laughter. Justin and Amalphia are both there on the screen, both looking really young and really rough, like they're hungover or have been out in the rain or something, make-up having run down both their faces.

"I actually knew that was there, Hearst," Amalphia says, in no need of a microphone to fill the room with her stage voice. "And I had almost complete control over this wedding... so, just keep clicking."

Will clicks on, and a photo of him in drag appears. "It was one of the kids' plays; the girls made me up," he explains as picture after picture of the same occasion turns up. "Fuck's sake," he mutters scrolling through them quickly.

The guests, or audience (everything this family does always becomes theatrical) are in stitches.

Finally we get to happy images of Justin and Kian together; Will toasts the 'obviously meant for each other' grooms, and then it's onto a Portuguese swordfish stew, Kian's favourite – vegetarian option available.

Keaton, whisky in hand, gives an intensely boring speech; I can't pay attention to it. Presumably he's done okay, though. Everyone claps as dessert wine – non-alcoholic alternative available – is passed round by the waiting staff.

Amalphia's on her feet again, mike in hand, weaving her way along behind all of us at the top table to address the hall.

"Before we move on to the desserts," she says, "which are very special – be excited – there is something vitally important I have to do." She looks back towards the grooms. "Justin and Kian got married today. It's so wonderful it makes me want to cry. But I won't." She flashes a naughty smile at Justin. "Marriage is a serious commitment," she says, indeed very seriously. "So some things will have to change. I need to ask certain people to give certain things back now."

She pauses. "Can I have a hat?" she asks, and the old woman in the wheelchair holds out hers which is basically a large red bird's nest. "Perfect, thank you, Madame," proclaims Amalphia, taking the hat. "You know who you are," she continues, searching the room with her eyes. "Those of you who have keys to Justin's house in London? Or his room here in the castle? And even the back door of our house? I have to ask you to return them now that he's a married man."

Crispin Truelove is the first to react; he comes forward and drops a key in the hat and gives a little bow towards Justin and Kian. Everyone laughs.

"There's a couple of peasants I need to see too." She says this directly into a camera. Presumably the whole thing is being broadcast on the big screen outside too.

Pasha and Colin, old dancer friends of my father's, or as Will calls them, 'the Ballet Bromance,' enter from the foyer waving little keys. Justin shrieks with laughter and claps his hands. I'm kinda surprised that they're here as I know Amalphia doesn't like them, but she's not one to bear grudges. She helped Pasha get some role in a film recently after a knee operation went bad.

"Good boys," she tells them now. "You get to stay for dessert."

She looks round at the top table. "Some boys are less keen to give up their keys, I see." She walks slowly along, and for a moment I feel resentful that she didn't give me one to hand back. Maybe I was too young to be included. Or too much part of the family. All the kids are everyone's kids, something I've always been keen to point out is factually incorrect.

She's stopped by Will now – the room waits with baited breath – but no, she moves on. No way. Papa Zolotov? I can't see him being willing to join in with this game.

He stares her down for a moment and then reaches into his jacket pocket and returns a key, all the while maintaining eye contact with her. She continues to stand there expectantly. He looks annoyed, but eventually rakes in a trouser pocket and plops a second one into the hat. She makes a big show of examining the keys she's collected, then glares back at him, and he removes a third key from his sock. The hall erupts with laughter.

Justin's on his feet, champagne glass in hand. "Phi, what can I say? You're a very naughty girl!" Turning back to the hall in general, he raises his glass, "I'll never forget any of you! You can still write. Email. Send your best 'special' pics!"

Kian's laughter looks as genuine as everyone else's. I'm not quite sure how I'd feel in his place with this game.

Some music starts up fairly quietly, but it must have relevance because Justin jerks his head round to look at Amalphia and she smiles back, that wide loving smile that we all know so well.

"Time for sexy, sexy desserts; I was told to say that bit," says Lexi, standing up with the twins.

Waiting staff wheel large dessert trolleys round the hall, offering a huge choice of puddings and cakes. They all have meaning, as my three siblings explain. There's chocolate cake ordered in from a café in Covent Garden.

"Justin introduced Mum to that cake long ago, and she's never looked back," Sophia tells us. "If it influenced the cake-mania thing she has going, well, thank you, Uncle Justin. It's enhanced all our lives."

The 'smores trifle,' I know well. Faye and Anna invented it one Bonfire Night, as Anna announces to the hall now. There's green jelly snakes that go down well with the kids in the hall, something to do with Keaton, I think. Cranachan, made of Scottish raspberries, oats and whisky and cream, but I'm no longer listening. I'm feeling a bit fuzzy again, to be honest.

The music gets louder, and something's happening between the round tables of the hall. A flash mob. Wow. She had dancers hiding in among the guests? Or are they just guests that happen to be dancers? But when did they rehearse this? And where?

Justin's screeching and clapping and explaining something to Kian. The choreography is strange, very obviously sexualised with much gyrating and sliding up and down each other. I notice Simone sneer and say something dismissive to Ross. I hate that she knows stuff that I don't, that she has memories and understanding that I'm missing out on. And that she's still here. I hate that too. Ross needs to escort her away out of here soon.

But why wasn't I involved in this dance thing? Why didn't Amalphia use the studios here to get ready for it? I told her she could use them for her and Ariel's Saturday classes, but she said no to that as well.

Anger surges down my arms, and my fists bang on the table. Nobody notices or cares. I force myself to breathe. It's Bevan's wedding. She won't forgive me if I fuck it up. Or would she? Where do I really fall in the pecking order of Treadwell's love? Am I really one of her kids? Or an injured stray like Pasha? Or something else entirely?

She's looking at me with a worried frown. This is not how I want her to see me, so I smile and raise my glass to her. Her happiness is restored, and what does that mean? That I have power? That I can make her feel happy or sad? That her love for me is different in some way like Justin asked me when he showed up here all angry and punched me that time? He said something about different... differently... something.

I'm too fuzzy to work anything out. I eat a jelly snake and watch the rest of the dance, the flash-mob, the entertainment, and, I guess, I am entertained. I am diverted and distracted from the mess that is my head anyway.

12

THIS PART OF THE wedding reception is over. People are moving. Tables are moving. I have to move. There's going to be drinks by the swimming pool. I see Amalphia talking to Madame. Faye and Anna are hanging off Will's arms, asking when they get to dance.

"Wanna go upstairs?" I ask Lexi. "I've put in games and stuff."

He wants to go. We're going, heading out the door of the great hall. But, in the foyer, Simone... what's the word? Saunters? Staggers? She would think it was something sophisticated like 'sashays,' I bet. But it's really more like: slithers. She slithers up to us in her crumpled red dress, hair blonde again, her minder, Ross, nowhere to be seen.

She holds up her champagne glass as if in toast. "A Manteith is back on the throne of the castle," she says. "All is as it should be."

"Isn't it about time you left?" I ask, staring her down. "I can't believe you were actually invited."

She shakes her head. "I'm here with Ross. His guest. But it's a bit odd, though, isn't it?"

"Yeah," I agree. "It is. So leave."

She grabs my arm and leans forward, her face close to mine. "Michelle, my mother, your mother, such a strong feminist, leaves her property and ALL her money to the male heir by default? The younger child?"

"The better child," I say, though I'm not sure I believe it. I mean, in my own way, I'm as fucked in the head as Simone.

"I looked after you all those years," she says. "I should get something."

"You really wanna go there?" I ask. "You want to start a conversation about that, here, with cameras going about everywhere?"

"There's no speaking to you, is there?" she snaps. "And I'm more your mother than you know. This lot won't have told you everything." And with that, she pushes past Lexi and me and walks, slithers, whatever, back into the great hall.

I kinda wish I hadn't mentioned the cameras because now I'm uber aware that they could be pointing at me, and I'm still walking about in my hop-shuffle-tap way. I've been trying without the stick when I'm here by myself sometimes, but it's messy and would be really noticeable today.

Just as Lexi and I reach the stairs, there's Clinton. And Henry. And everyone I kicked out of the castle basically.

"Are you going up?" asks Ariel. "Because we could do with a bit of quiet for the babies?"

So I'm in a little crowd of my own now, flanked by my brother and, amazingly, my friends.

"What you done with my bedroom?" asks Clinton.

"Nothing," I say. "It's still there; you can stay in it if you want."

"Might take you up on that," he says, and up we go.

⁓ele⁓

They're all impressed with the upstairs studio and the purple sofas and screens and stuff. The babies get laid out on one of the fluffy blankets, all in a row. Alex with an x looks cool, in a tiny shirt, all smart for the occasion.

And I've got toys for them now. Rattles and teddies and musical things. Jonasz is well impressed that I did that.

"I'm not a totally selfish bastard," I tell him.

"Never thought you were," he says. "Living and working with your family? Dude, I get it. It can be too much sometimes."

But I need to find Bubbles. She's the only one who's not up here. The only one of my class, my friends, my... she's something different too. Someone I really need to be up here with me. So I go in search of her. And food. I need to find food. We need snacks upstairs.

I step-shuffle my way down the stairs and into the foyer. And I see Bubbles at once. She's speaking to Aiden by the big front door. American Aiden. Crispin Truelove's son, or 'love child' as he kept calling himself last year. Him being beside Bubbles means I have to invite him up too.

They accept my invitation and head to the stairs, and I'm about to go with them when I notice Amalphia standing by herself at the back of the room. And I know by the big-eyed look of her that something's majorly wrong.

"You okay?" I ask and she jumps before turning and seeing that it's just me.

"I keep running into people who shouldn't be here," she says. "Something must have gone wrong with the guest list, or the invitations. Sadie's with an ex of mine who... Well, it wasn't good. Long time ago now, though. Maybe he's changed. I hope he has for her sake."

"Where are they?" I ask, looking round the foyer for Sadie, friend of Simone. I remember her. I don't like her or trust her, and she most definitely should not be here. On Justin and Kian's special day. In my castle.

"It doesn't matter," says Amalphia. "But don't tell Aleks or Will. I don't want anything nasty to happen at the wedding."

"You're shaking," I say, taking her hands in mine. She's really pale too. "What did he do, this guy?"

"There was one incident where I thought I was going to..."

"Die?" I say, knowing it's true by the state of her. Been there. Know what that's like. I can feel the effect and the atmosphere of that type of abuse as I look at her.

"It's alright, Alexander," she says. "I'm okay. Now."

But she isn't. And I want to save her from it. "A few of us are taking a time-out before the dancing begins," I tell her. "Upstairs. No cameras. No one who shouldn't be here. Want to join?"

She frowns. "Oh. Well... perhaps for a very short while."

Upstairs it's all quite loud. But still a haven from people like Simone and Sadie and whatever scumbag they've conjured up to torment Amalphia with today. Because I remember how they liked to do stuff like that.

"These are nice," says Amalphia in the upstairs studio, running her hands over the corded fabric of the largest sofa. She sits down. "Cosy."

I take one of the purple fleece blankets and wrap it round her. "Suits you," I tell her because it does.

"Being distressed and coddled? I've spent a bit too much of my time here like that!" She laughs but snuggles back in the blanket. "This is a great space, though, Alexander. I like it very much."

"It's a place to chill," I explain, seeing that all my old classmates are doing just that, Bubbles still ensconced with Aiden. "Actually, there was something I wanted to ask you," I say to Amalphia.

"Oh?" She looks interested, and I know this will take her mind off the bad stuff.

"Would you be all right coming upstairs? To your old room?"

"Okay," she says. She looks a little unsure, and brings the blanket with her, but she accompanies me up the stairs to the room at the top of the tower. It's slow, with my ankle, and once we get there, she sits on the bed which used to be hers and is now mine.

"Found this old map," I tell her, fetching the faded brown thing from the ensuite where I left it. "It shows how the castle and grounds used to be. The castle's smaller, but the stone circle is the same, look. Your house is like a shed or something."

She smiles. I knew she'd like seeing the stones.

"But here's what I wanted to ask you about: the Deil's Pool. See how it's so much bigger? That stream at the side of your garden flowed right into it back then; it doesn't do that now. I was down looking at it; there's lots of boulders and rubble that seem to have been used to reroute it."

"Oh, yes." She looks at the map and traces her fingers over the words, *Castle Loch.*

"I would like to fix it," I tell her. "Put it back how it should be."

"Go for it," she says. "It'll be good for you to be outside. Too much time spent in this building does not lead to good things. Not in my experience."

"I need your permission," I tell her. "The boundary between the properties is right across the middle of the pool, and it'll change the stream. It'll veer away from your garden much earlier. If I manage to do it right, that is."

"Do it," she says. "You know, it makes me think of Jackie, the wise old man who used to live in our house. He told me that putting things back where they ought to be in the landscape changes the places around them. Corrects the energies. I had the missing stone put back in the circle after, well, after bad things that happened here."

"The stone that fell on Michelle? The one that disabled her?"

She jerks her head up from the map, shocked, I think. She looks straight at me.

"Yeah, I know some of that," I say, rubbing her arm and looking directly into her eyes.

13

My dearest, dearest boy,

I need to speak to you of dark events, terrible things that I wish had never occurred. I would rather gloss over them, rather you didn't know. It can only distress you, only cause dismay. But I cannot risk that you would come to doubt Amalphia, or believe her to be unjust in her hatred of me. We've told you of that hatred already, of course. Well, Simone has. Threatened you with it actually, and for that I am sorry too.

But the truth is that Amalphia has every reason to hate me. I dragged her into the lowest parts of the castle and tortured her. I can imagine you thinking that must be figurative, not literal. I wish it were. The details, I will not give you. That would only demean her. I was ill, psychotic. I do not remember any of it, but my doctors told me in great detail. The scars on her body are my doing; they were not caused by an accident, a story I've heard told since.

I believe, in my madness, I was connecting back to my own abusive childhood. I was projecting onto her. Learning of her relationship with Aleks was not a good moment. He paraded it in front of me as if he knew of my unhappiness but, arrogant fool that he is, he imagined me to be jealous.

Amalphia exasperated me. Her anger, her autistic bluntness. And her talent; well, that is undeniable. You think I mean danc-

ing? Acting? No, I talk of my research, and her latent abilities which were only lightly touched on. How far we could have taken it, her and I, if left to ourselves to work and communicate clearly without his constant presence. He distracted her away from what mattered. I didn't understand it then. I don't begin to understand why she's still with him now.

I hope it is not to do with the damage I did, the harm I exacted on her. If I could go back and correct one thing, that would be it. Maybe, in this one way, I can. If Amalphia is separated from Aleks now, that can only be good. She would be free to enjoy her relationship with Will. They are a wholesome pairing, their little ones so beautiful too.

Twin children born of twin souls. I allow myself the odd romantic notion here at the end of my life. It is good to think of love working out, and being only good, untainted by ugliness.

So bear no grudge against Amalphia because you saw me stay hidden from her. She has every right to loathe me, and to distrust anything that comes from me.

Despite this, I would like her to know that I am your mother. Indeed, I would like to be the one to inform her of this, and to be able to do so in friendship, but I can see no way that would ever happen. Simone has promised never to tell her. If the task falls to you, I know you will do so carefully and with due consideration and kindness. But do not risk your relationship with Amalphia. It is precious. I would not want her to look at you in horror. I hope, when enough time has elapsed, that this will not be the case. You may have to judge that for yourself.

I know she had the stone that fell from the dungeon ceiling and crushed me placed in among the moon stones afterwards. That may have been a celebration of my destruction. I don't know. I am not in a position to know what Amalphia thinks of me now.

I'm sorry for this bleak inclusion in my letter to you, but it had to be done. I shall try for a more upbeat subject next time, I promise.

Michelle

———·*ell*·———

It's disappointing that Amalphia's so keen to get back to the wedding after seeing the old map. I'd hoped she might want to hang with me a bit longer. Maybe I spooked her by talking about the dark stuff, but I want her to know that I'm in on that secret now. She doesn't have to keep up the accident story we've all been told. Not with me anyway. And I kinda wanted to keep her in the tower, safely away from the guy who hurt her, the guy that Sadie brought along today.

I want to know more about this guy, though, so I join Amalphia in the elevator and head downstairs with her. She goes to find Justin and Kian, and I start my investigation.

I search the crowd in the great hall, but can't see Sadie anywhere. I haven't seen her since I was a kid, so I can't properly remember what she looks like.

And what did this dude do to Amalphia, exactly? He nearly killed her. But how? Not in some sort of traffic accident. Why would she be so shaken up to see him then? It has to be something else. Something worse. Something much worse.

The anger is icy cold as it travels round my body. It needs to be put to use. Later, though. Once Justin and Kian have set off on their honeymoon. Once it's just guests dancing and drinking and enjoying everything she's prepared for them today. Then the one who doesn't deserve any of it, the one who shouldn't even have been here? He can be dealt with. I punch the side of a large speaker beside the stage that's been set up for the band, but keep the movement small and unseen, or at least, I think it's unseen.

"What's up, cousin?" asks Ross, stepping down from the rostrum. "I wouldn't pick a fight in here. Phi'll string you up."

"Someone needs sorting," I tell him, knowing he'll understand that.

"It'll have to be much later then," he says, only telling me what I already know. "And preferably outside. Find a girl to dance with; have a drink. But first…" He plugs in a mike. "Amalphia Treadwell to the stage. Is that right?" he asks her as she emerges from the crowd and walks towards us. "Is that what they say in the big Hollywood fillums?"

"Don't get mouthy with me, McCulloch," she says, stalking over and taking the mike from him. "And no, if it's a film that Crispin's in charge of he tends to shout, 'Hey, Treadwell, we need you over here in the mud!' or something like that." She flashes a wide smile in Truelove's direction as the audience, guests, whatever, laugh. "We still have to have that talk," she reminds the actor, and he beams back.

Amalphia continues: "Well, Justin, here it is. You're still sure you want me to do this? It's not too late to call it off? This particular item, I mean; you're married, no getting out of that one now."

I think she's still rattled about the guy that came with Sadie; she's doing that babbly thing, and I know she hasn't been drinking. She's still really pale looking too.

A shiver goes through me. I'll have to ask Will about Sadie being here. He'll point me in the right direction.

"Get on with it, Treadwell!" yells Justin, and she does.

I'm fucking floored. I mean, I know how talented she is, and that she can really sing, but it still gets me every time.

The old song that she's singing suddenly becomes my new favourite song. The dancers from the flash mob are in on it too; she dances with them all over the hall, and with random audience members too. She pulls Will across the floor by his tie, and squeezes herself in between him and my dad while dancing with them. I think she's trying to feel safe. I just know it. I'm not doing the eye-blurring thing for that – that would be way weird – but it's over in a second. And then the song is over too, and I'm like: Oh! Everything's dull and sad now.

And I need to take a pill to kill the pain. Again. So I do. In fact, I take two.

14

KIAN AND JUSTIN HAVE their first lovey-dovey, waltzy dance together, and lots of other couples join them on the floor.

"Beer," says Will, appearing at my side and handing me a green bottle that's bound to create a nice buzz to make things more bearable. "How you holding up?" he asks. "Having your new home invaded like this?"

I shrug. "How you holding up with Bevan staying and everything?" I know Justin and Will have never really got on that well.

"He'll be gone soon enough," he says, looking over to where Amalphia is adjusting Justin's bow tie and speaking quite intensely to him.

My father is watching Amalphia too, from the other side of the hall. He's leaning against the wall, trying to look cool.

"Is this the day he's gonna explode?" I ask.

"Huh?" Will looks confused.

"Zolotov. At me, for everything."

Will laughs. "That's not gonna happen. You've hardly been home, so you don't know. But you've kinda set him free. And her. They've got travelling plans. And all these ideas for working together. They're like a couple of excited kids sometimes. And I love them for it."

And he's totally serious. It seems out of place with the rest of Will. He's such a straight guy, but he'll snog Zolotov. And other stuff; we all know but don't speak about that: the three of them together. But I guess no kids like to think about their parents having sex.

But back to the business of the afternoon: "Is it right that Sadie's here?" I ask him.

"Is she?" he asks, looking astonished. "See, this I don't get. I understand that Bevan wants everyone to see him get married in a pink fairy-tale castle among the stars. But he's invited people nobody wants to see. Simone? I mean, really? And we definitely could've done without Sadie."

"She's with some prick that Amalphia used to date." It's out of my mouth before I can stop it, and she asked me not to say anything. And I've clearly just ruined Will's night.

"Who?" he demands.

"Someone who hurt her, like physically, I think." There's no shutting me up today. I don't have a name which is probably just as well because in my 'two pill' state I'd have blurted that straight out too. Though I don't seem to feel fuzzy right now; if anything, I'm wired like I'm hyperactive or something.

And the search is on. Will involves my father, who immediately takes on the appearance of a human thunder storm. The two men debate who Sadie's mystery guest could be. Three names are bandied about: Luke, Ciaran and Gavin, though they both doubt it's the last one, Gavin. I'm really uncomfortable with all this. Knowing there was one violent guy, one douchebag, was bad enough, but there were more? What did they do to her? She made a date-rape documentary a few years ago. I hope it wasn't something like that. I'm shaking, like she was earlier.

"It's all very serious over here," says Amalphia, putting an arm round both of her husbands as she arrives beside us. Flashes go off behind them. From cameras and phones. She rolls her eyes. "We're totally open, we've given interviews, but still they seek to be the one who exposes us. I could've done without the press today, but Justin wanted them here, good publicity and all that. But, what's up with you boys?" She eyes us each by turn.

"Sorry," I say. "It just sort of slipped out. About Sadie being here..."

"Oh, I think they've gone," she says. "I haven't seen them since we came back downstairs. I told him he should leave."

"Told who, exactly?" Zolotov's words are more clipped than usual, his accent more pronounced.

"Gavin Tuesday," she replies, and this gets a big reaction from both men. "He could be a changed person for all we know," she goes on. "He seemed to be being all sweet with her, with Sadie."

My father: "The fact that he thought it was appropriate to show up here—"

Will: "Yeah, what the fuck? He needs sorting, Malph—"

"No," she almost shouts. "No sorting of any sort. No spoiling Justin's wedding. And think of Sadie. Will! She was in love with you; you can't go wading in and punching her boyfriend for no apparent reason. How would that look? She undoubtedly doesn't know about that stuff back then... and it was so long ago anyway. He's no threat to me now."

She persuades Will and my dad to dance with her. More cameras and phones are raised.

I lean back against the wall, and then I see Sadie. It's like the crowd opens up to reveal her to me. I remember her vacant face from a long time ago, a bad time ago. And she's with a guy, a tall and dark-haired guy. Not really Amalphia's type then. They're keeping to one of the shadowy edges of the room, though I think Sadie's trying to convince him to dance. He looks at his fancy watch. He says something that makes Sadie frown. And then he sets off round the edge of the hall, keeping his head low. He seems to be heading for me.

"D'you know where the toilets are?" he asks, like he has a right to speak to me, to speak to anyone here, to speak at all.

I point into the kitchen passageway, and he sets off up it. There is a small toilet up there some way back, but I'm willing to bet he won't find it. Guests were meant to use the ones in the theatre corridor today.

I wait a few moments, then check that no camera is focused in on the 'bad boy of ballet,' and I follow the loser into the dark passage.

I find him quickly. He's standing looking into the room with the glass floor, the door to the underworld of the castle. He's lit up by the green light of the room as he stands in the corridor and peers into it. The green light makes him look like the monster he is.

I feel sick with rage as I run at him and push him and he tumbles down the steps and into the room, saying something like, "What the—?"

And then he's lying on the floor, the glass part of it. Lit up green from below. And he's: still. Still. As. Fuck.

I walk down the steps and stand over him, examining the idiot who hurt Amalphia. I shove his leg with my foot. There's no response. She gave him the right to touch her and he abused it, abused her. I bend down to examine him, and I see that he's still breathing. Even though I hate him, I know that's good.

So, what to do? What would teach him a lesson? I look round the small room. A stone angel gazes back from the wall, its hand pointing downwards. See, I know this is like an ancient signpost to the underground tunnels but here, today, the angel seems to be pointing to the old drawer unit. I pull a few drawers open and find a roll of heavy-duty silver sticky tape and a scissors. As used in the 'big Hollywood fillums,' as Ross would say.

I cover the monster's mouth with tape. It's harder than it looks in those films. The tape keeps sticking to my fingers. I do his eyes too; don't want him to see me if he wakes up, do I? Then I bind his wrists behind him and then his ankles, round and round. It reminds me of the time Lexi and me built a fort with boxes, back when we were kids. We used so much tape, and forgot to leave a doorway. Amalphia had to cut us free with scissors. Her face appeared between boxes, smiling, opening the way to freedom and safety.

The guy's legs are heavy as I lift them to bind his ankles which are sweaty under the grey trousers. Hairy above his stupid white socks. That tape's gonna hurt when it comes off.

But he won't be hurting anyone anytime soon. She's safe. I'm keeping her safe.

15

I MAKE MY WAY back through to the great hall, and I see Amalphia at once. She's talking to Crispin Truelove, right at the other side of the room.

She sees me. I smile. I try to. I think I smile. People move out of her way as she crosses the hall.

"Speak to me," she says. She's so kind. How can anyone have ever wanted to hurt her? "Alexander," she adds, like real stern. "Tell me what's happened. Now."

"I've done something stupid," I admit. "That guy. Gavin. I've got him all tied up in the green-floor room."

"What?" She grips my arm and pulls me back into the passageway.

I tell her the whole thing. It's like I have no off button, no mute, no silent mode today.

"Is he hurt?" she asks.

"He was knocked out at first, but he's woken up now, and he's thrashing about a bit."

She studies my face, her own face white as a ghost again. "Why did you do this?"

"He hurt you. I couldn't just let him get away with it. I mean, that just... I didn't mean to go so far, though. I was really just going to punch him, but then... It all just got away from me."

Her eyes are big in her pale face. I start to explain better, but she stops me. She shakes her head.

"Let me think, Alexander." She pauses a moment and seems to be forcing herself to take deep breaths.

"I've made things worse, haven't I?" I realise.

She shakes her head again. Maybe she never stopped shaking her head.

"We're going to fix this," she says, very determined. "Did he see you? Did you speak to him?"

It's my turn to shake my head.

"Show me," she says. "But stay quiet. We don't want him identifying you."

So back we go, along the passageway to the glass-floored room. I open the door and we look in. There he is, just where I left him. His head jerks up at the sound of the door. He makes a small noise. He goes quiet. A dark patch appears on the crotch of his trousers and spreads downwards; a pool forms and grows on the glass floor, the liquid lit up from below and glowing like it's radioactive or something.

Amalphia stands frozen beside me. Her hands are cupped over her mouth and nose and her breathing is ragged now. I pull the door shut and she looks at me, lowering her hands and beckoning me up the hallway a bit.

"I shouldn't have told you about him," she whispers. "And you shouldn't have done what you did." She looks at me, for agreement, I think.

"I know," I say "I was just so angry."

"Okay," she says, and then, "Okay," again. "We need to let him go, and we need to protect you. However, you must promise me that if you ever want to do something like this again, you will come to us. Any one of us will help you with what you're feeling and discuss if anything needs to be done."

I nod my agreement to this. She makes me promise not to move from where I am, and tells me she'll be back in a minute.

I do what I'm told. I lean back against the cold tiled wall of the passageway. And breathe. And wait. And wait some more.

And then she's back. And she's only got Crispin Truelove with her!

Crispin eyes me warily. "I'm really not sure I can go getting mixed up in—"

Amalphia interrupts him. "Do it, and I'll give you my written permission for your ridiculous film."

"The film is not about you," he tells her.

"Polyamorous people who live in a castle?" she counters, eyebrows raised.

"You don't live in a castle."

"With twenty-seven children?"

"You don't have—"

"There's a case there, and you know it," she tells him, then rethinking. "Do it and I will tell people, any media people you like, that you're the greatest actor I've ever known. Carry this off, and you will have proved it to me." She holds out a knife to him. It's small, like a cheese knife, I think. She's not shaking now. It's as if arguing with Crispin has pulled her together or something. "Let's get this over with, shall we?" she says.

He stares her down for a moment and then shrugs. He seems to be agreeing to whatever plan she must have suggested because he takes the knife. His face changes, as if he's become another person. I've seen this happen before, of course, but here, today, it all feels unreal, like I'm watching them in a film and I'm not really here at all.

My head is spinning. My world is spinning. I wonder what terrible secret I'm now going to be sharing with Amalphia and Crispin – I mean, it involves a knife – and I follow them down the steps into the glass-floored room.

Amalphia mimes for me to be quiet. Both her and me slip our shoes off. Crispin keeps his on and stamps about a bit.

"Look at you, lying in a pool of your own piss," says Madame, the woman with the large hat, who Crispin has just become. "Useless. Quite useless."

Gavin's head raises but he stays quiet. The tape over his mouth makes sure of that.

"So you've had a little scare," says the Madame/Crispin person. "And a little tinkle. But is it enough to answer for what you did to my favourite student? My dearest Amalphia?"

Gavin stays still.

"How could you think it was acceptable to come here today? To show yourself in front of her? In front of me? You scoundrel! No, I think a little more teaching has to take place. Only then can I consider you properly trained."

Madame/Crispin runs the knife down her/his prisoner's cheek, gently so as not to actually cut him, and Gavin begins to make whimpering sounds behind the silver tape.

Amalphia holds up her hands to Crispin as if to say, 'That's enough now.' But it's too late.

Crispin Truelove is deeply immersed in his role of 'Madame alone in the dungeon with her prey.' He pokes the knife into Gavin's back.

"Do you even deserve to live?" asks Crispin.

Gavin begins to shake, like really shake, and makes some noises like he wants to speak.

Crispin continues to speak in Madame's voice: "But then, maybe if you promised never to hurt any woman ever again? To worship at the feet of sweet little Sadie?"

Mad nodding from Gavin is the answer to this.

"I will find out if you break your promise, but, oh!" Madame sounds sad now. "I suppose I should let you go. I don't really want to, though; what fun we could have."

Crispin runs the knife up Gavin's leg, stopping where the trousers show dark and wet. Amalphia grabs his arm and shakes her head at him.

"You're lucky it's the good voices I can hear today, Mr. Tuesday. They say I should undo your feet. No kicking, though, or I get to play." He cuts the ankle tape away with the knife.

Amalphia uses wet wipes to wipe over the tape that's left: hands, eyes, mouth. Crispin drags his victim to his feet.

"Okay, my pretty," says Madame. "Up the steps we go."

Crispin coaxes Gavin up the steps and down the hall, poking him with the point of the knife as they walk. I follow, and then I open the back door of the castle for them. We all shove Gavin out the door and triple lock it behind him.

We run back up the corridor before we speak. I run too. I can feel my ankle hurting, but I run anyway. I don't know where my stick is. I don't know where I left it, or when I abandoned it.

Crispin is himself again. "Treadwell, I can't believe you involved me in what I think has to be some sort of felony—"

"You were only meant to let him hear Madame's voice and let him go," she says. "No one will believe it was her. And she actually left a while ago, so his story will lack any credibility at all. But you weren't meant to do more harm."

"The role took me," explains Crispin.

"Well, your involvement in this is over," she tells him. "Go back up the way to the foyer. Alexander and I will enter the great hall separately soon, and then we will all behave like we've been there all along. It'll take him a while to find his way round the side of the building. There are lots of trees to confuse him. He's in for some fun taking the tape off his eyes. But I have a good idea what to say when he does appear. Don't worry, Truelove, you'll get your film and your acclaim."

Crispin leaves, and Amalphia bends over, hands on her knees. "I feel like I've just performed a very long ballet," she says, sounding out of breath.

"I'm sorry—"

"There's no time, Alexander. We don't want people to notice we're missing."

So we return to the great hall. She goes in first and heads straight for my father. I watch from the entrance to the passageway as she holds onto him and closes her eyes. He hugs her back, concerned, I think.

Right. Time for me to step into the party again too, among all the pink glitz and flowers, but it's hard to act like nothing's just happened. Because: what the fuck did I just do? What did we all do? It's mad and disturbing, and I think my pain meds are wearing off. I sit heavily on a chair at the side of the room.

Amalphia sits down beside me just as Will announces over the mike: "The grooms are going to chuck their bouquets now. All single people should gather in the foyer!"

"This is perfect," says Amalphia, taking my hand and walking across the hall with me to the foyer where there's a crowd of excited people waiting for the bouquets. "Everyone will remember us being here," she whispers. "And we're being filmed too."

Justin yells from where he's standing on the wide stone stairway, "The term is toss, Hearst, not chuck! We're going to toss our bouquets. Everyone shut your eyes and turn around on the spot."

We do. It's super disorienting. I feel dizzy and a bit sick. And then Amalphia, beside me, is suddenly holding a bouquet.

"No!" shouts Justin, storming down the steps. "You're not stealing my thunder this time, Treadwell. You've already got two husbands. Two! Leave some for other people, won't you? Go and stand over there. Go on!"

Looking suitably chastised, and having been very well-noticed, Amalphia moves to the back of the crowd.

Bubbles catches Justin's flowers on the second throw.

"Cool," I tell her. "Anyone I should know about?"

"As if," she says, looking up at me, all pink and pretty and bright, like the opposite of everywhere I've just been, like the opposite of me really.

"Maybe I should ask her?" says Aiden, all loud and tall on the other side of Bubbles.

She laughs as sparkling pastel confetti falls from the ceiling like snow.

Justin and Kian soon hold all attention as they sweep out the door and into their fairy-tale, horse-drawn carriage.

We all follow them down the steps and onto the gravel. We all wave them off. Amalphia cries. Whether that's about Justin leaving or what I did in the green room, I don't know. My father holds her again. Ugh. I don't blur my eyes to imagine that's me instead of him, but they seem to be all blurry anyway. I feel like I can't see straight.

Then someone in the crowd shrieks: "Oh my God! There's a... man! I think he's gagged or tied up!"

He is both of those things. A stupid, disgusting, vile, evil man is staggering round the side of the castle, silver tape still over his eyes.

16

I CAN'T BELIEVE HOW cool Amalphia is acting about what's happening. She stands silent and open-mouthed like everyone else and lets Sadie be the one to rush forward and start taking the tape off.

"Something terrible has happened to Gavin," Sadie tells us after conferring with him. "He was assaulted and tied up on his way to the toilet!"

A waiter comes out of the castle and announces that sandwiches and coffee and hot chocolate are being served in the great hall and the marquee. I remember Justin calling the marquee a massive erection, and I sort of want to laugh or to be back in that simpler time, a time before I'd done this latest fucked-up thing.

There's a small crowd out here, watching the Gavin drama, my whole family included. Sophia whisks Faye and Anna away back inside when she sees what's going on. That's good. They shouldn't be near this. This mess I made.

Someone suggests brandy as Gavin sits down on the steps by the front door. My front door. My steps. Justin and Kian's brandy from their wedding, I'm guessing.

"I think he's had enough to drink," says Amalphia, gesturing at Gavin's wet trousers. "You say someone tied you up?" She sounds incredulous. "How did you get away?"

"She let me go," he says. "It was, I mean, I think it was... Madame."

"Madame?" says Amalphia. "Our old teacher, Madame? A woman who is disabled now and in a wheelchair."

"No, no." Gavin looks confused. "There were two of them."

"Two Madames?" she asks.

He nods. "They kicked me down some steps."

Amalphia is now playing the part of someone who thinks there is no more point discussing the matter. "Maybe we could get some strong coffee for Gavin?" she requests of the waiter who's stayed to watch. "A sandwich too; it might help soak the alcohol up."

Gavin glares at her, a high level of aggression clear in his face. I know he's not a changed man, and he would hurt her again if he got the chance.

"I was assaulted," he says now. "And you need to call the police."

"That is the correct thing to do when someone's actually been assaulted," she says, giving him a hard stare.

Sadie looks a little troubled, but she stays quiet.

Amalphia continues questioning Gavin: "So, apart from Madame, who always loved you, is there anyone you can think of who might bear you ill will and want to do such a thing to you? You know, something for the police to seriously investigate?"

"Madame went back to her hotel," says Will, standing next to Amalphia. "I put her and her carer in a car a couple of hours ago."

"And it is time to do same for Mr. Tuesday." My father's not-to-be-argued-with teacher voice is, well, not to be argued with. I always hated that voice until this moment. Now I see its usefulness. "You have had much to drink from the open bar at this wedding," he continues, looking at Gavin with obvious disdain. "You have fallen down some steps and banged your head. You dream of old women doing things to you." I have to hand it to him; he's making that sound super sleazy. "Is time to sleep it off, I think."

Gavin says nothing, but he eyes me suspiciously, perhaps remembering the toilet directions I gave him.

And then Simone appears in the big old doorway of the castle and stares down at everyone on the gravel. She's shaking with laughter. "Gavin and Sadie, Gavin and Sadie," she sings. "You always did want Amalphia's leavings, Sadie!"

"What?" says Sadie, looking at Gavin in question.

"Ancient history," explains Amalphia as Simone skips down the steps and starts twirling about on the gravel.

"Where's Ross?" I ask, knowing that he usually tries to keep an eye on Simone and prevent this sort of thing. I mean, it's bad enough that she's even here. At least she could try to behave.

"He's eating a ham sandwich," Simone tells us as she walks over. "I had one too! It was just lovely—" She stops walking suddenly as if she's hit a wall. "Oh!" And with that, she projectile vomits on Sadie.

Amalphia organises us all. Holly takes Sadie away into the castle to clean her up. Will is told to call a taxi for Gavin and Sadie; he then offers to wait outside with Tuesday.

And, as we all make our way back to the great hall, it seems like it's all over, as if it never happened. I'm just a normal guy walking into my normal castle on a normal day in my normal life.

Amalphia's all over Zolotov, smiling up at him, sheepish, the first sign she's given of having been up to anything. She holds his hands and dances along in front of him, backwards across the great hall, all the way to the wedding cake where she proceeds to pop a giant chocolate from it into his mouth and then one into her own.

The lights dim, and dancing begins again. Slow stuff, romantic stuff, but I can't see Amalphia anywhere anymore.

And then I notice the phones. A few people are pointing them in the same direction, towards the furthest back wall behind the buffet tables. Fuck. She's only snogging the face off my father. I mean, really eating him alive.

And then they're speaking, and speaking. People get bored and lower their phones. I wait for the kissing to start again, because I don't want them to be speaking about me, and it seems likely that they might be speaking about me. They stop speaking. Good. And now they're coming this way, and fast. Not so good.

"We're heading back to the house to put our feet up," Amalphia tells me. "You come over soon, Alexander. And I expect to see progress on the pool, though do try to balance your time there with the stone circle. The pool can be dark and creepy, a bit like this place. But being outdoors will be good for you."

She has her arms round my father, but she's concerned for me, like she's being pulled between the two of us.

Amalphia's voice is a whisper: "The gaslighting thing we, well, I, did to Gavin out there was a terrible thing to do. It's actually a very bad thing, an abusive thing, to mess with someone's reality like that."

My father puts his hands on her shoulders. "You were triggered by the presence of an abuser here on what should have been only a happy day. His past actions were the cause." He smiles at me, an unforced smile apparently with no agenda. "Well done, Alexander," he says. "I told that man long ago that if he came near her again much worse would happen to him than a punch."

"Aleks!" she chides, not wanting me encouraged into any other weirdness, I assume. She looks back at me. "I'm going to message Sadie and tell her what he was like. I suspect she won't welcome my input, but at least she'll be warned and will recognise any red flags when they happen. Oh, here's Will."

Will has somehow hurt his hand when he was outside with Gavin. She kisses it and shakes her head. She establishes that Gavin and Sadie have gone. And then they're gone too, all three of them, Amalpcia, my dad and Will. I stand on the top step outside and watch them head off through the woods together.

"Must have been quite an experience growing up in that family," muses Crispin at my shoulder.

"I guess," I say.

"Quite a story there, I would imagine?"

He's fishing for information, and it's annoying. And anyway, he's wrong. "It was all really normal actually," I tell him. "The more interesting parts came before, you know, when I lived with my, you know, Simone." Now I'm annoyed with myself. Simone is not 'my' anything. And she's not interesting.

"Dark stuff," surmises Crispin, correctly. "We all have it. We like to keep it tucked away, but it can be what makes us, sculpts us in the end. And... shall we get a drink?"

I know that he's not really my best friend, but as we sit down at the rose-petal-strewn table in the great hall, he makes me feel like he is.

I talk. I drink wine. I bleat stuff about Simone that I haven't thought about in a long time. Then there's the radiator. I've never told anyone about that, but Crispin gets the full story tonight. It's 'a real doozy' as he says. I hope it hasn't sculpted me.

"Don't you use your own experiences in your art?" he asks. "Your acting?"

I correct him: "I'm a dancer." I correct myself: "I was a dancer."

"Have you forgotten the documentary we did here? And that face, those eyes. Well," he says, seeming to cut himself short. "It's something for you to think about. I know you're between jobs – resting, we call it – but if you ever feel like a career change, I could show you the way, open a few portals for you."

The rest of the night is a blur, a very peculiar blur. At one point it seems as if we're walking down 5th Avenue in New York – it's sunny daytime there – champagne glasses in hands. Then we're sitting on a Californian beach watching a golden sunrise. He must be telling me stories, and making them feel real or something. His acting can transport you; I've heard someone, possibly Crispin himself, say that; maybe his words can too.

We exchange private – he makes a big thing out of this – phone numbers. I drink a hellova lot more wine.

Then I feel sad and also panicked to see everyone leaving the party and the castle when I've just come back from the States. Wait. State of alcohol + pills + Crispin's stories, more like.

So I persuade people to stay, to choose bedrooms for themselves, to help themselves to food, and tell them they can swim in the pool whenever they like.

Alexei takes the room below mine. We're brothers at the top of the tower. Princes. Kings. I dunno.

Clinton, Paul, David, Keaton: they're all staying too.

Ariel and the babies and Jonasz left long ago when I was... wherever I was.

Bubbles and Henry go too. They don't leave together with Aiden, though, and that's good. He really strung the two of them along last year. And I would hate for that to happen again. He exits the castle on his own tonight.

The grooms' dads leave; I don't think anyone ever found out which was which.

Ross takes Simone home and then comes back to stay with us all.

It seemed like it was all over, but I think party time at the castle has actually just begun.

17

THIS MAY ACTUALLY BE the happiest I've ever been. There's a perfect order to my days. I get up and eat breakfast in the big castle kitchen. Sometimes Holly pops in to make sure everyone's eating properly. I say I should pay her for this which offends her.

She cooks bacon and eggs and black pudding and mushrooms and potato scones for us all. I say I'll get fat; she points out that I'm a 'skinny-ma-link.'

I head outside early in the morning. The others are all still in bed. The eternal partying wore thin for me after two days, but they're still going strong, if gaming and drinking and eating takeaways can be called strong.

I stand by my pool in the woods ready to reclaim it from the deil or devil of its name. Its modern name. It's time for the Deil's Pool to become the Castle Loch again. A place where mermaids swish their tails and comb their golden hair.

It's dark in this bit of the woods, especially this early in the day, but I don't find it creepy like Amalphia does. I'm mesmerised by the reflections on the surface of the water; sometimes the pool is like a mirror, a perfect glassy pond showing an upside-down version of the silver-barked trees. Other times, it wears waves like a choppy sea. But it's too small. Someone shrunk it long ago, for what reason I don't know, but it was wrong. It feels wrong to me that that was done.

There's all sorts of artefacts among the rubble that was used to redirect the stream. I put them on a table in the dungeon studio as I find them, and that underground room becomes my own personal museum. I put the coloured glass together; maybe there'll be enough at some point to join it all up like a jigsaw and see the bigger picture or object. There's some massive stone bricks, parts of a building, I think. I gather the blocks together by the pool. I find a huge metal candlestick and decide to use in the kitchen to eat by at night.

That worries Ross a bit, the candle thing. He's always seen himself as some sort of older brother or protector in my life, and him staying here with all the others only seems to have amplified that idea. I know he's 'keeping an eye' on me. It's vaguely annoying, as if he's watching to make sure I don't go nuts like Michelle at her crazy worst.

"I'm diverting a stream, not studying people's brains," I tell him over my candlelit ready meal. "And I'm not a drooling lush like Simone."

He doesn't like that. He reminds me: Simone can't help it, she's not quite right; we have to look out for her.

"I owe her nothing," I say and storm out of the castle, slamming the back door of the building as hard as its weight will allow.

Anger eases among the trees. The water looks brown today and is dotted with those small yellow leaves of the season; it's a good combination, the brown and the yellow.

I walk on by the pool, pull on my working gloves and get to work on the stream. I feel like I'm doing proper, real work. No tights, no music, no dusty studio. Just me and the woods. Me and the stones.

It's a much bigger job than I realised, though. There's just so much rubble, and so many great boulders to be shifted. Realistically, I'm gonna need Ross's help for some of this. The stream has not moved an inch so far.

I stand on the big stone in the pool, for a rest really. And then I find it. I find her.

A beam of sunlight shines through the trees just as a flurry of golden leaves spirals down onto the centre of the pool. And I see a face, for a moment, down there in the depths.

I have to go in, to wade right in to the very middle of the water. I can't see the face anymore, having churned up the water and the mud, but my foot soon hits her. I know it could just be a rock I've found, but at the same time I know it's not. I submerge myself totally and see her face through the gloom of the brown water. I scrape at the mud and the twigs and the years, decades, centuries of muck that has settled on top of the rest of her. At first I think she's a mermaid, but then I see her crown and the baby that she's holding. I've found a mother.

One quick text to Ross, and he's there, using a small tractor to haul the stone statue up and out of the water. He's excited. She could be historic and valuable, but whose land was she on? Which side of the pool?

I don't care. I won't be selling her. I summon everyone else to look, but most of the party people are not interested.

Faye comes through the woods from the house and gazes at her, at the statue. Amalphia and Anna come too.

"It's the Virgin Mary," says Anna, bored and unimpressed, and off she flounces back to her ballet practice. I recognise unfortunate shades of my father in Anna. Even at seven years old.

The others stay and admire the lady a little longer. Faye, especially, is very taken with the old statue and fetches toothbrushes and soap to clean it up, so I end up just giving the thing to her. It goes well in what is now her room alongside the ancient bed and harp from the castle.

Amalphia jokes that the room is turning into a museum; I can tell that she's pleased I've given Faye this piece and she promises to visit the pool again soon.

———ele———

I sense the change in the forest as soon as she steps inside, and she does every day. Amalphia. The place loves her. Even the birdsong changes, becomes chirpier.

She lays out a picnic on a stone at the side of the pool. There's always a flask of hot chocolate; on colder days there's soup too. Today there's chocolate donuts and cheese softies, those floury Scottish rolls I love so much. She smiles, and silver branches dance in the breeze.

We always talk as we eat: what's happening at the castle, what's going on at home. How's Alexei doing? She misses him, I can tell. It's odd for her, him being at the castle. And me, how am I doing? Good? Really?

I accept her invite to dinner. I take a box of chocolates from the village shop with me, and it's actually really, properly good to be home.

"So, it's just me and my girls?" I say on hearing that both Will and my father are away. So are the students; they're away off home for their October holidays before they go on tour. That's a bit of a shame; I'd hoped I might see Bubbles.

Anna's not happy; her dark eyes flash in annoyance. "Papa should be here to teach me," she says. "I might develop bad habits if I practise too much on my own."

I end up giving her and Faye a pre-dinner basic ballet class upstairs in what I think of as Will's studio. They enjoy it; I may have started something. Though, over dinner, the family's bigger plans come out.

The men are off in London starting some 'collabora-tive and innovative' dance project for young people. Both Emotzia and the ballet company that Amalphia and Will used to work for are involved.

My girls – that's Faye, Anna and Amalphia tonight – are going to head down that way soon too. Amalphia's doing a 'collaborative and innovative' – she laughs – film project with Justin.

The more I hear about this second project, the more I feel she's being 'taken the loan of' as Holly would say. There's no way she'd have agreed to such a bizarre film if it wasn't Justin's idea.

"But it's all going to be so easy," she explains on hearing my doubts. "I waltz round London eating cake and meeting people in cafés. Aleks and Will are to be in it sometimes too. The main character of the film is a man who's obsessed with me and making an unofficial documentary about me. I play myself being stalked, basically."

I can't see the humour in this. Michelle was obsessed with her and spying on her in secret. I remember being asked to hide listening devices in the house when I was a kid. How can Justin think this is appropriate?

"Don't worry," says Faye, as if seeing into my mind. "Dad will look out for her. I wish I was in it; I think it would be fun."

"Hmm…" I say, very glad that she isn't involved.

My protective instinct has been activated, and I stay the night in my old room in the house. It's a little embarrassing to admit after my big break for independence, but this really does feel like home. The house is warm from the sun; that never hap-pens in the castle. Well, maybe in the upstairs studios, but only occasionally. There's the smell of home baking and soap and wooden floors here. The castle has those things, some of them, sometimes, but the air doesn't hold onto them or wrap them round you like a cosy blanket.

And I don't dream here. I just sleep. Like a log. Properly. Literally. I wake up in exactly the same position I went to sleep in. Not sweaty. Not heart thumpingly. Just still and relaxed and calm.

I like the feel of being the man of the house. I like having breakfast with them all, despite Anna's constant complaints about everything. Amalphia jokes that her daughter is a dark-haired Goldilocks, but in Anna, I see my father's temperament hidden within a physical likeness of Amalphia. What a dangerous combination.

It becomes a thing, my staying here at the house. Every third night quickly turns into every second night. My last vestige of pride stops it being every night. How would that look to my father? Like I'd moved back home? And I haven't. The castle is my place. The woodland pool, too.

I feel parts of myself opening up beside the water. Beside the pool. The evenings bring unbelievable sunsets. Pinks and oranges and purples appear over the gnarly silver birch tops. I run through the woods and up the hill – I've not used the walking stick since the wedding – my feet making a new path to the stone circle. From there, I stand atop the biggest stone, the one that lies down, the recumbent, and look back over the tops of the pines. They make a dark and jagged base for the colourful display in the sky, and I stay there until it fades.

Ross says the pines are mature now and that they need felling or thinning which could be profitable. But I don't think Amalphia would like that. And this is really her place, whatever deeds and wills might claim. I arrange for the branches to be trimmed back on the pathway, where they might impede her visits. I know she comes here at night sometimes. Often with Will.

Maybe one day, her and I will meet here? Not this day, this night, though. She's gone – all my girls are gone – away down south to make films, and play in the city.

Realisations come between these stones, so she's told me. I visit them a lot.

18

ONE MOMENT I'M TIED to a radiator, being burned, lines of fire on my back, wishing someone would break into the house and kill me just to end the pain. Then, like always in this particular nightmare of the past, there's Simone's laughter and Simone's voice: "Like mother, like son."

I thought she meant me and her, that's what I thought back then when the actual event – her tying me up to 'keep me out of mischief' while she was out – happened. But now I know that she must have meant Michelle, my actual mother. But how was I being like Michelle? It doesn't make any sense. It never did, then or now, dream or real.

I wake. I reach for my phone, and as my eyes clear and my back cools, I see Amalphia on the screen, Amalphia everywhere, in fact. Her name's trending on every social platform going. It looks like something messed-up has happened with the film thing in London. I don't look too closely because as soon as I see the photos, I know I don't want to see her like that. No one should see her like that.

I can see that she's being hounded by the press, though. I can tell that from the photos that members of the public are posting of her. One of the pictures was obviously taken at an airport.

Where was she going? I bet I know where.

I get up, get dressed and head straight out of the castle and through the woods to the house.

And there she is. Sleeping on the sofa in her sitting room. She's hurt. Really hurt. It looks like she's got a broken ankle. It's got a cast on it like mine did. I didn't see any mention of that online. Her forehead is covered in little dots of sweat, and she's kinda grey looking.

And she's obviously all by herself in the house. Really? I mean, what the fuck? Maybe my father or Will have nipped out to get food or whatever, but for just now, it's just me and her.

I put my hand on her face to see how hot she is – very – and she wakes.

We stare into each other's eyes for a few moments before she struggles to sit, wincing as she moves. "Oh, Alexander, I'm so sorry," she says.

"No. What for? You haven't done anything wrong."

She shuts her eyes and leans back on the couch. "I've done everything wrong, and screwed things up for everyone. I'm really sorry about this, but could you get my bag for me? I think I left it in the kitchen, and I need painkillers."

I get her the bag and a bottle of water and then watch her down the whole thing in one go after she swallows four pills. Really good ones. Prescription things like I was given for my ankle when I first hurt it.

She starts listing the things she's ruined: Justin's film, which is rubbish as it wouldn't have existed without her; Aleks and Will's project. Again, rubbish. If the company have really pulled out of that like she's saying, then they must have already wanted to. I tell her what total cunts the management are known to be there, and her eyes widen at the word.

"Sorry," I say.

She shakes her head. "I remember what they're like. But the children. The little girls will see it all online, and David and Sophia; at least you and Alexei are older, but it must still be embarrassing."

"No," I say, trying to convey with my tone how strongly I mean it. "You haven't killed anyone, have you? Just visited a, well, a..."

"A sex shop. Yes."

And she tells me the rest of it. And I'm horrified.

She only went into the shop because she thought they were Justin's guys that were following her, actors for the film. But they weren't. So two sleazy reporters watched her do what she thought was a humorous skit with adult toys, and then they chased her down the street and into the tube station. They watched her fall over and break her ankle. They filmed it and smiled and waved. And then she got a cab. By herself. When she could hardly walk. When, like me when I broke my ankle, she should not have been walking at all.

"You went to the hospital alone?" I ask, incredulous. "Why didn't you call someone?"

She looks confused. "I didn't think of it, but they were all working, busy, you know."

"You're more important than any work."

She looks right at me and lands the clincher, the doozy, the final nail: "You know the last thing Aleks said to me? He told me he was tarred by his association with me."

It bubbles deep down, the rage, but I keep it there, tucked away, out of sight as she talks on confusedly: "I was a bit out of it with the shock of it all and the painkillers. I might have picked it up wrong. Maybe he meant... The company, I think he was actually talking about them and their association with him and Will... I don't know. I don't remember properly..."

I study her. What does she need in this moment? "When did you last eat?" I ask.

"Umm... I think the cake before it all kicked off yesterday morning, but it's mainly thirsty that I am now."

I fetch her more water and make tea for her and give her a bag of chocolate buttons like she used to do for me when I was small and hurt. That almost makes her smile. But she's not herself. She's dreamy and sad and keeps staring into the distance.

"Do you ever visit the chamber?" she asks, pointing at the picture over the fireplace.

That painting always freaked me out a little when I was a kid. It shows a baby curled up, like it's been buried alive in the earth under the stone circle. And umm, yeah I have visited it, but not recently, so I tell her: "I prefer the stones, and my pool."

She squeezes my hand. "I was so angry when Ross showed it to you, the chamber, I mean. You were only fourteen. What right had he to take an innocent child down there into the dark? I was going to wait till you were much older. But maybe it's better that it didn't come with everything else, you know, the will and the letter. There's only so much change and weirdness a person can take at a time." Her words rush out in a fast stream which seems to exhaust her. She switches to slower more thoughtful speech: "Sun says it's a place of retreat and rebirth. See how it's shaped like a womb?"

"Ross never said anything like that," I say, laughing. "He was like: there's this secret place in our family, your family and mine, the McCullochs and the Manteiths. He was real precious about it – told me we had to keep it hidden away – like it was a holy shrine or something."

Now she's looking like she might cry. "I need to hide away just now. That's where I want to go. Will you help me get there?"

"Of course," I answer at once. "But are you sure? You could stay in the castle. We'd look after you. Alexei's there too, re-member. Or just stay here. I can stay too."

"There," she says definitely, pointing at the picture again. "A retreat from the world," she continues. "I can fast, drink water, clean out. I need that. I'll come out reborn and stronger, a better person."

"You don't need to be a better person."

"I don't want to see anyone, Alexander. Will you please not tell people where I am? We might need Ross's help, though; I'll need access to the toilet in the basement of the cottage. I can shuffle up the steps on my bum."

We don't need Ross; I help her.

There's no way she can go down to the chamber from Simone's cottage as that will involve using an old metal ladder to get to the basement. So I use a sledgehammer and open the tunnel from the basement of this house for her. It's quite fun, as it goes. The brick wall my father had built is demolished in half an hour.

We walk down the small staircase and along the tunnel together. It's hard going on crutches for her.

Then she wants to lie on the cool stone of the floor of the chamber with no bedding or cushions or anything.

"You're going to regret that," I tell her and insist on leaving a duvet and a camping mattress and two pillows there.

I stockpile some water and food bars in a corner. She gets me to light the candles. They're big thick ones, so they'll keep going a while. The entrance with its huge boulder isn't airtight, so she won't suffocate, but I'll be checking on her regularly anyway.

I spend the next forty-eight hours running up and down the tunnels at odd times of day and night and spending a lot of time in the basement of the cottage too. I like knowing that she's just below, with me, her guard and protector. Simone, in her home above, never ventures down here.

One time when I sneak down into the strange little chamber, she's lying there all peaceful and quiet, curled up in my duvet, only her broken ankle and foot sticking out. I know she's going to need a proper meal when she emerges, which I hope will be soon, so I head up the tunnel to the house to see what there is in the freezer. I can go shopping for fresh stuff later, once I've checked on her again.

I click the basement door shut behind me and stand in the hallway of the big house and immediately feel the change that's happened in my short absence.

Angry tension is detectable in the air even before I see the furious form of my father striding towards me from the kitchen.

19

"WHERE IS SHE?" HE demands. "Have you seen her?"

I sense he doesn't suspect that I just entered the house from the basement, which is a good thing.

"No enquiries about her wellbeing, then?" I say.

"What?" He's livid. He looks almost rabid. "What?" he repeats, his voice a growl.

I push past him, and go up the hall into the kitchen, wanting to get away from that door in the hall in case he realises it's a clue.

He visibly seethes as he stands before me by the big white kitchen sink.

I keep my cool. "Why are you even here if you're so concerned about her tarring your reputation?"

"What?" he says, looking confused as he takes a step towards me. I don't move an inch, don't even flinch. "Where is she, Alexander?" he asks. "At the castle?"

"She doesn't want you to know where she is."

It's great to see him lost for words and bursting with rage at the same time. I want him to be the one to hit first. I really want it. Despite being angry with me many times over the years, he's never hit me, never hit any of us. I've never seen him this furious, though, so I tense with the anticipation of it, and squeeze my hands into fists.

He pretends he's still holding it together and tries to sound calm, like he's the voice of reason or something. "You must tell me where she is."

"Why would I let a jealous bastard like you near her?"

"Jealous—?"

"Yeah," I say, taking a step closer, squaring up to him properly. "You're jealous of her success." I poke him in the chest. Everything in him tightens and readies for the fight. I land a series of pokes with a series of facts: "You discourage her, tell her she should be here more, being a good little wife to you, don't you? You're happy enough to take her money, though, aren't you?"

He bats my hand away, and it's all the in I need. I go to punch him, but he blocks it. I use the other hand, but he bashes that away too and pushes me back from him.

"We are to talk of jealous now?" he says with a bitter smile, walking away from me. "All truths bared? Who has an inappropriate crush on her, Alexander? Who gazes from the corner?"

The sick bastard. I charge and knock him down and then find myself flying forward; I sail right over the head of him, landing face down on the slate floor. That works out quite well; I manage to kick him in the face. He twists on the floor and holds my legs.

"You think she will be glad to learn of your secret feelings?" he says. "It was cute when you were a young boy, but now it is just wrong."

The scorn in his voice sets me on fire. I move like lightening and I'm on him at once. The punch connects with his nose with a crack. Bullseye! But fuck, he's strong; in a second, it's me that's pinned to the floor under him, my hands held back behind my head while he sits on my belly. I kick out like a stupid little kid in a playground scrap, but I can't move.

"You will tell me where my wife is now, or I phone the police!"

Blood drips from his nose and lands on my cheek. It's warm. I look up into his face, contorted with anger as it is, and I spit upwards. A wrestling match develops as he tries to contain me; his elbow gets me in the eye. Fuck, that hurts.

There's a loud, "Fit the—?!" and Holly joins the fray. The sad thing is there's no disobeying Holly, so when she tells us to sit, one at either end of the long kitchen table, that's what we do. "Man, oh man, oh man," she says, hands on hips, shaking her head in disgust.

"Have you seen Amalphia, Holly?" he asks, trying to sound like a sensible, decent human being.

"No. Fit why? Is she up here?"

"Alexander knows where she is, but he won't tell me. She's injured and upset, and I need to see her."

"Should have thought of that two days ago then, shouldn't you?" I say, wanting to have Holly know the whole truth of this. "She broke her ankle and made her way to hospital alone. Then she travelled across London on crutches by herself and went home and got your dinner ready! And you were a right cunt to her. She told me all about it."

Holly looks from me to my father. Blood is congealing under his long nose. Some of it got in his hair during the fight. And he's still fighting, fighting to keep his temper in check, that is.

He takes a deliberately slow breath. "When Amalphia is want to hide something, she is very good at it," he says. "I did not know of her injuries until the girls told me this morning. She said she needed her space, so Will and I did not see the crutches or the cast; she seemed well to us. We realised later she had been acting, and we have tried phoning her repeatedly, left many messages, as have Justin and Faye. You must tell me what you know now, Alexander."

Holly's gaze settles on me. I study the triangular notch on my end of the table, run my finger along its sides. Okay, I'll tell what I know. "When she arrived here, all by herself, she had a broken ankle and a high temperature. She was exhausted and distressed. She'd been through a humiliating experience. An experience everyone knows about." I pause and make a decision. "There's no mention of her injuries in the press. I wonder if they actually happened after everything, you know, when you were so pissed off about your precious project."

His breath hisses. "How dare—"

"Would explain why she doesn't want you anywhere near her, wouldn't it?" I say.

"I would never hurt her."

"That's really not true, is it? Seems to me she puts up with pretty much anything from you." He stares back but doesn't speak, so I continue. "When stuff goes wrong for you, she's all support, isn't she? Woman turns up with an unwanted bastard kid of yours? Amalphia's right there for you. She has the most shit day in history, and you're all: 'Oh no, how vill this affect my crappy leettle project, my attempt to prove I still count in some pitiful—'"

"Enough!" roars Holly, breathing out in exasperation. "You twa boys have your issues, but this is not the time for 'em. Amalphia's safe?" she asks me, and I nod. "She's had medical attention?"

I nod again. She did in London.

"Aye. Well, yer needin' a steak on that eye, Alexander. Aleks you can make yer own sweet way to the hospital to get yer nose seen to."

"I am not leaving here without—"

"I've got this noo," Holly says to him. "She'll phone you when she's ready to spik to you."

She calls a taxi for him. There's a big awkward silence during which we're given tea. It's sweet, not as sweet as Will would have made it, but quite sugary all the same.

"I made tea for her," I tell them, remembering that moment, and her gratitude; the way it was me that took care of her for once. "She hadn't eaten."

"Really?" says my father, but his voice has changed. It's all soft and worried now.

"She was dehydrated too, so I gave her water. And pain killers. And chocolate buttons." I'm not sure why I'm offering quite so much information. It just burbles out of me.

"Good," he says. "Good."

He goes, but with the air of someone who's going to head straight back ASAP. Holly and I watch the taxi drive off with him.

"He would never hit her, Alexander," says Holly. "He's a bit single-minded and thoughtless sometimes, but nae that. So, I take it she's doonstairs in the chamber?"

I stare at her in wonder.

"Makes sense, laddie. She's not at the castle, and she'd be in the stones, but it's raining."

She is not pleased to hear that Amalphia has been underground for two days, but before the conversation gets any more heated, the doorway in the hall opens and the woman in question falls through it and onto the floor.

20

MY DEAREST BOY,

I'm sitting in my room staring out at the trees as they sway this way and that in the wind. The night has turned fierce. I sense a similar change in you since you learned about your father. Oh, you're perfectly polite to me, too polite, as ever, but there's a new wariness, and I hate to see it. It hurts. I don't know how to correct it, how to remove this invisible distance that now exists between the two of us.

All I can do is write to the man you will become and hope that he, you, will understand.

How could I tell you? You were keeping enough secrets. It was easier for you to enter their house not knowing your paternity, not knowing quite what you were to them. Or was it? Am I telling sweet stories to myself to assuage the guilt?

I wanted to be the one to convey the truth to you and was furious when Aleks insisted it be him. And then it wasn't him that did it. I felt enraged again when I learned that she had been the one, enraged at his cowardice! But now I can see she was the best choice; she made it not only bearable, but a fun little outing, chocolate and all. She even had you smiling, something I see far too little of.

I feel the question as if it's time travelled back to me, through the veil of death. How did I see that, you may ask? A hidden camera, my dear, as ever. I know it's unacceptable to many. But you see the clearest truth about people when they don't know you're there. When they think they're unobserved.

Which means I saw you all the next morning too. I watched you play with your siblings. You are a natural leader. Aleks's other son veritably worships you! I loved to see you play with the twins too in the safety of Amalphia's caring gaze. We watched over you together, or that's how it felt. And then I listened to her explain to him how to be a parent. Though maybe she was explaining to me too; it seemed as if she were speaking to my heart. For too long I thought of you as a means to an end, not a child, not my boy as I know you now.

But no longer. I love you, Alexander. You are my flesh. You are my heart. I hope the other telling, the bigger one, will be easier, and I hope it will be me that tells you that I am your mother. I know haven't behaved like one. I hope there is time yet to correct that.

The light has faded while I've written. The sky is dark grey, the branches of the trees black against it, whipping and whirling in what may be turning into a gale. I feel like them: dark, the wholeness of what I am in shadow and unseen, blown about by a situation that now feels out of my control. I could lose you completely. I hope I won't. The thought causes me to weep and shake like the trees.

Don't keep secrets, my son. Not from anyone you love.

And I do love you.

Michelle

⸺

Holly and I lift Amalphia off the floor and support her through to the kitchen. She obeys Holly, just like we did, when told to sit at the table. She leans her elbows on the old piece of furniture and laughs.

"Noo, fit in the world do ye find funny, quiney?"

"So many things," says Amalphia. "Falling over like a clown. Being called quiney. Surely I turned into a wifey a while ago?"

"Nonsense! You're the bonny quine ye've always been. Isn't that right, Alexander?"

I'm about to say: yeah, of course that's right, when Amalphia sees me and looks horrified.

"Alexander! Your eye! What happened?"

"My father, that's what happened."

"He hit you?"

"It was more like his elbow caught me—"

"Rolling aroon the floor like twa bairns, when I came in," Holly informs her.

"Because of me?" she says. "But why was he here? Where is he now?"

"I've sent him off to hospital," said Holly. "I think his nose was broken."

The cup of tea would have been better if Will had been here. As it is, I make it while Holly starts to prepare soup.

Amalphia decides it's time to look at her phone. I sit by her at the table to be supportive. She's quiet as she reads her messages. Then the internet flashes a foul image up on the screen: Will's been photoshopped into some sort of sexy underwear she was seen buying that day. There's even the headline: *Where Is She Now? The Hunt for Treadwell is Go!* The same article includes a request to the public for photos of her and her family.

She stares out the window at the silhouettes of dark leafless trees against a grey sky.

"You're shivering, Phi," says Holly, wrapping a blanket round her shoulders.

I get out the chocolate biscuits.

Amalphia stays silent as she starts to listen to her voice messages. "One problem at a time," she says, and she calls someone on her phone.

"You hit him?" she asks the person on the phone, and I like how cross she sounds. "I asked you a question. What? Alexander helped me. He was only kind and thoughtful."

Seems to be going quite well for me, this conversation.

"Talk later? Make that much later!" she shouts into the phone. "You go back down south, Aleks; that's where your priorities lie. Stay away from me. These messages from you and Will could be from twenty years ago, right back at the beginning: the two of you against an idiotic Amalphia. I have enough to deal with. Give me my space."

There's a listening pause.

"I'm not a frigging angel! I'm an increasingly angry woman. Leave me alone!"

She disconnects. "Crispin has messaged that I should answer the press, put my side of the story out there too. He knows how to sort this kind of stuff." She dials. "Answer your phone, Truelove," she whispers under her breath. And he does. And he talks her into going over there, to the States. All of a sudden, and without thinking it through at all.

I call Lexi, and get him over here from the castle. We all eat soup together and try to talk her into staying. I mean, surely she shouldn't travel in her condition? It doesn't work.

Soon an enormous black car with dark tinted windows appears in the driveway, and it carries her away. And the trees sway in the wind, dark and lonely, jagged against a colourless sky.

21

THE NEXT TIME I see Amalphia, it's on TV. I'm between Bubbles and Ariel in the theatre, my theatre in the castle. It's a bit surreal. Alexei is lolled a bit further forward. Clinton is fiddling with the massive screen on stage, a smart screen, recently installed, meaning that I'm a guy with his own cinema too, I guess.

"Try it now," says Clinton.

Henry throws something from his tablet, and we've got it. Well, we've got adverts, but we're going to watch Amalphia live on American TV with Crispin Truelove. She's gonna be discussing what happened to her, and I can't wait. My whole body buzzes with excitement like all its processes have been sped up. Heart: faster. Brain: quicker, alert, sharp. Muscles tensed, ready to run. Which is a bit stupid really.

"We should do this more often, for happier reasons," says Ariel, having already told us that Alex with an x is doing well, gaining weight and ticking developmental boxes on the health visitor's list, which is well awesome.

"It would never have happened to a man," says Bubbles in a loud voice.

We all look at her, confused.

"Amalphia," she explains. "If Will or Mr. Zolotov had been filmed buying sex aids, the press would've been like: 'Go them! What a dog!' But because she's a woman, well, how dare she suggest she has needs or might take the lead in bed, like ever?"

I nod, because, yeah, that sounds about right.

"And she's so fantastic," adds Bubbles, and that's definitely right. "There's been no mention of all the counselling work she did here, has there? Where would I be without her? I'm going to write her a letter, Alexander. Could you get it to her?"

"Of course," I tell her. "Will's going out there to see her soon, so he can take it."

"We should write to the papers too," says Ariel. "Amalphia helped me so much when I first came here. She's so down to earth. That day when everything went pear-shaped and I had to move out of Jonasz's parents' house: she grabbed the 4X4 keys and took me to get my stuff. Gave me cake first. Took me for lunch after. She doesn't behave like she's mega-famous and important at all. And she's autistic. Has there even been any mention of that?"

"Let's dim the lights," says Lexi, interrupting, and getting up. "Like we're really at the movies. It's fitting for Mum."

So, there, in the dark with my brother and my friends, I watch my stepmother – the woman I have an enormous crush on, according to my father – hold a pink vibrator high in the air and then drop it on the ground like a mike drop. Seriously. That's how the show starts. But it gets better.

Sitting in a bright studio with Crispin for this TV special, she tells the gruesome tale of the day when she was hurt. How she had thought that the two guys following her were Justin's actors – a smiling picture of Justin appears on a screen behind them – and that it would be fun to go into a sex shop. For comedy reasons. And it really does seem funny. We're all laughing along with her, as is the studio audience in America. Grainy photos from papers appear on the background screen, none of the really nasty ones, though.

People in the TV audience are shown to be crying when she tells the story of the train, how she got out of the carriage when she realised the men had followed her in there too, how she fell, how she was injured, and how they just kept on filming. She's blushing, looking really unhappy as she says all this.

"Nobody helped you?" asks Crispin, incredulous on hearing how she struggled through the station to the taxi rank outside.

"A man did help pick up my things. It was unfortunate that so many of them were from that shop!"

Crispin shakes his head. "But an injured woman was left to fend for herself and then derided in the press. So you flew away to the heathery hills of Scotland?"

"Yes, I stayed with my eldest son for a few days."

Me. I blush. I feel a bit hot and uncomfortable. I'm really not sure I did right by her either, leaving her down in the chamber all that time when she was unwell and hurt.

Crispin goes on: "Would you say the incident and the following press coverage put a strain on your relationships? Your marriage?"

"Yes," she says with no hesitation. "Absolutely. My husbands were involved in a dance project and a major collaborator pulled out after the incident, not wanting to be associated with anything sleazy. You know, me."

"Was that this company?" Crispin asks, an image of the company's London theatre appearing on the large front-of-studio screen. "A place where you, yourself, worked in the past?"

She nods. I nod.

"Is anyone else thinking it?" he says, turning to the audience, and they clap. "Who wouldn't want to be associated with this lovely lady, this star of stars?" He takes her hand and kisses it.

Amalphia's wearing a sparkly dress. It glitters and shines under the bright studio lights.

"And then this happened," says Crispin, indicating the screen which has now filled with the front page headline, *The Hunt is On!* Crispin's face is a picture of disapproval as he says:

"But it's not the only hunt that is on. You were hounded and harassed by two men. Chased from your own country, no less. Would these be them?"

We're shown a photo of two men hiding behind a red telephone box.

"Yes!" shouts Amalphia. "That's them!"

"The independent film crew you were working with spotted them several times while going through their own material," Crispin tells her. "These guys have been tailing you for a while, honey. So, it's over to you," he says straight into the camera. "It's time to name and shame. They deserve it. Use hashtag #AmericaLovesAmalphia for messages of support in the meantime."

Live messages scroll down the side of the screen for the rest of the interview, and we're told that the hashtag is trending immediately as is #CrispinLovesHerToo, started by the man himself during the show.

Crispin then speaks at length about his new film and how Amalphia is working on it in an advisory capacity, keeping the polyamory all above board and correct.

"It is so wonderful to have my dear friend staying with me," Crispin said. "And now: we're having a baby together!"

"What?" says Amalphia, at least that's what her mouth seems to say, the sound is drowned out by the cheering and clapping and whooping of the crowd.

"Yeah..." drawls Crispin, milking the moment while all of us in the castle theatre sit in stunned silence thinking stuff like: well, she did have a baby with Justin, so maybe... "It's not true," says Crispin finally. "We're just very close friends. But that's how rumours are born. Let's see what the papers do with it."

And with that, the programme ends. It's followed immediately by an advert for *A Wedding at the Castle* which is going to air over Christmas, and then an older film starring both Amalphia and Crispin comes on.

Clinton and Henry break out popcorn and cola, and we watch Amalphia, as the Fairy Princess, resist the wooing attempts of the Prince and the Most Handsomest Man in the Land, the latter played by Crispin. She was my first pin-up girl, that fairy was. When I was newly up here, I had a poster of her on my bedroom wall at home, in Amalphia's house. I watched the film and its sequel, like a thousand times.

"Here's to Amalphia and defying the patriarchy," says Bubbles, raising her cola in the air, and we all cheer.

22

I LOVE THAT SHE phones at the same time every day. I look forward to it; butterflies form in my belly in the half hour leading up to the appointed time. The nights are drawing in now, so it's always about sunset when she calls and I describe the colours in the sky to her, as well as the trees, the growing pool, and the changing reflections as the light fades.

She tells me that her world is currently totally constant: the sky and pool are always blue, and Crispin is still the same age he was when she first met him about twenty years ago. She's growing tired of his publicity stunts, though the two guys who harassed her have been found and charged. So, that's good. She likes that I'm always outside when we speak; she says it connects her to the places she misses.

I make sure to be in the stone circle when she calls sometimes, and I tell her how peaceful it feels, but that the place misses her too.

I laugh and smile. It's the only time I do now. The castle has become a sad and hollow space. Everybody has basically left and gone back to their lives. Bubbles and all the other third year students are away on tour. I watch them on the school blog, which is still up and running. Bubbles is the shining star of that show.

Lexi's still here, most of the time, some of the time. Ross looks in now and again to ask me what I've been doing, suggesting I need to get a life. But apart from them, I'm alone.

The old building is quiet as well as cold now. It's not a good combination. My imagination plays tricks on me at night; I think I hear distant piano and sounds of partying and dancing, laughing and even people having sex. How stupid is that? The top room of the tower is so far away from the studios and hall, it would be impossible to hear stuff like that even if it was happening.

But Amalphia's coming home for Christmas. That's definite. She's nervous about it, not sure how she stands with everyone, especially him, my father. So we make a plan: she'll mislead him about the flight times and come here first. We can spend the morning of Christmas Eve together with no interruptions from anyone else; I think Lexi can be persuaded to go home early without me.

We're going to spend some time in the stone circle, and then she can see the pool with the stream flowing into it. I hope she's impressed; such a fuckload of work went into it, she has to be impressed. I hope the weather's good that day so we don't have to cut our time outside short. And I hope my father continues to fuck up, big style, like the idiot he is.

I give in to the fantasy that she might stay with me in the castle rather than sleeping at the house; well, if her visit there is terrible, she just might. I buy stuff, so much sparkly Christmas stuff. Faye helps me put it all up. I don't let her go up the ladder, though, and get Lexi to hold it when I do, but it's so difficult to decorate up there at the ceiling level of the great hall, so only a small patch gets done. I don't think Amalphia will mind. I get a massive tree delivered and Faye lets loose with artistic expression. I tell her it looks like a drunken Christmas elf's been sick all over it, to make her laugh, but actually it looks awesome like it's been decorated by designers in a posh shop.

I do a great big online delivery of food, because though I know I'm invited to all festive activities at the house, I don't intend actually staying there. I might not even be welcome. I haven't seen him since the day I punched him. Neither has Amalphia, of course; Lexi says his nose is noticeably fucked up, more than it used to be. I don't know how she'll react to that. But she's coming here first, so she'll feel sorry for me all alone in my great big castle first, and he'll fade into the background.

The day arrives. I've never been so excited about Christmas or, as it actually is, Christmas Eve. Not even when I first came up here and was experiencing it for the first time with Amalphia and her family. I was always nervous then, unsure what to expect and what to do, just waiting to be accidentally inappropriate.

So today is different. Lexi is easy to convince that I'm wary of seeing our father and waiting for Amalphia to arrive before I head home, so he sets off for Christmas Eve breakfast at the house without me.

And I wait. Minutes go by so slowly. I almost wish I hadn't hired a company to clean the castle this last week; it would have given me something to do, some way to fill in the time until—

She's here! I hear the car on the gravel, and I wrench open the heavy front door.

She's so skinny and tanned, all movie-star looking in her big sunglasses (and it is sunny – score!) and hat. She's smiling at me, pleased to see me, and hugging me, so full of love (for me – score!). She tells the driver to get lunch at the hotel and that she'll tell him where to deliver her bags later. Triple Score. I wasn't wrong about that situation. She's not sure where she'll be staying.

"Can we run straight up to the stones?" she asks as if she needs my permission. "Would it be mad if I did it in bare feet? It would obviously – I can see that it's frosty – but I've missed this so."

She takes her boots and socks off at the foot of the path; I offer to carry them. She pushes her sunglasses up onto her head, and then: she's off! She's like a demented pixie or something, moving so fast, I can hardly keep up. I'm out of breath when I reach the stones; she's standing up on the flat stone, hands outstretched to the sun.

"It's just the same," she says. "So wonderful." And she lies down on the stone, undoes her long black coat and just kinda flops.

For a brief moment I wonder about squeezing on there with her, but it would be intrusive, maybe even aggressive. I'll leave that sort of mistake to him. She doesn't stay in quiet meditation mode for long; she's soon up and walking round the circle, looking at it from all angles.

"I love the way it looks in this low winter sun," she tells me. "Such long shadows and dark silhouettes."

"I haven't really noticed that," I say. "I'm usually here later on in the day, and there are no shadows. It's cool here then too, though, when everything's getting dark."

"Yes," she says in beautifully deep agreement with me. "Yes." Then: "Show me your pool, Alexander."

I can tell she's not too sure about the new path I've made, as if it's an unwelcome change to her stones. I point out that it begins quite a distance away from them and then realise she's just taking it all in, touching the trees, enjoying this different birch-lined walkway.

And then: "Oh!" She stops and stares at the pool. "Wow, it's quite different, so much better. Is it wrong that I want to get in and swim? The rock's in the middle now; I could sit on it!"

She comments on the silver nature of the water, no longer dark, no longer creepy. The trees that had been at the edge are now in the pool; I don't know if that will kill them. She's totally philosophical about that too, saying they'll either live or die, but the stream is returned to where it should be. She mentions that she would like to swim in the pool again.

"I'd better not, though," she says with a nervous glance towards the path that leads to the house. "There's enough potential for awkwardness without arriving bedraggled and wet and suffering from hypothermia."

"I've a present for you first," I say, delighted that I hid it here for her. She always appreciates thoughtful gifts that don't cost much money, and I hope I've gaged this one well. I nip behind the largest tree, the one that's all gnarly and thick, the one I don't think the pool will manage to kill, and remove the two broken slabs. "They must have been part of a bigger crest," I say, handing her the one with the carved stone mermaid on it. "She's like you, in your pool, on your rock."

"I think she's more like Bubbles," she says with a sideways smile at me, tracing her fingers over the carving.

I frown and move on to the other part of the gift. "I found a bunch of broken stuff around here, all sorts of artefacts. Here's the bear."

She smiles and takes the other piece of stone, holding it against the first one. "So now they're together," she says. "No underground labyrinth in between. That's nice. The bear makes me think of Aleks, big and strong and sometimes grumpy." And suddenly she looks a little older, no longer the ageless pixie running up and down paths in her bare feet, and I hate him for it.

She turns her big eyes on me and takes a deep breath. "Well, I suppose it's about time for the prodigal son and wife to return."

I laugh at the way she says that: son and wife. It sounds like she could be my wife who I'm bringing home. And in a way, I am bringing her home; she came to me first, and he won't like that. She puts back on her boots, zipping them up to the knee over her jeans. She does up her coat again and secures the sunglasses over her eyes.

I follow her through the wood. We pause while she notices that the little bridge serves no proper purpose anymore, and she seems to get further away. From me, at least. That feeling grows once we enter the garden. She looks around at everything then turns decisively and walks up the stone path and back to him.

23

I STOP AT THE foot of the steps because she's stopped. She looks nervous, standing there, looking in the doors, which are open. I smell wood smoke. I hear something too, the squeak of the stiff wood-burner door. And who's likely to be fiddling with that? Whose presence in that room has made her stop and look small and frightened? No guesses needed.

I walk up the steps to offer her support, but she steps inside before I reach her. He's bent over the fire. Then he's standing. Then he sees her. It's like the slo-mo setting on my phone's camera. There's nothing slow about his smile, though; it's over so fast, it's like it didn't really happen.

"Malphia!" he says like he's amazed to see her. "Ah, but you are early!" And he pushes his hands back through his hair, looking a bit annoyed to be honest.

"Oh," she says, taking a step back, uncertain of her welcome.

Time for me to step forward: "Hey," I say, standing beside her.

Then she's talking, real fast, like she has to explain herself: "Well you see, I came early and went to the castle and the stones first with Alexander," – she touches my arm – "I thought it would be about the agreed-upon time by the time we'd done that. And we went to the pool in the woods, and I wanted to swim, but I didn't..."

"Quiney!" Holly bursts into the room, closely followed by the multitudes, and everything warms up a bit in front of Zolotov's fire. There's hugs and cries of "Phi!" and "Mum!" Amalphia doesn't want to take her coat off, but Holly wins that argument.

"Aye, well, you're far too thin, ye will feel the cold!"

"I knew you were up to something this morning," says Lexi to me with a laugh. "I mean, I thought it might be woman related, but I didn't think it would be with Mum!"

Everyone laughs, well not quite everyone. My father continues frowning. Amalphia sits by the fire where she puts down her mermaid and bear stones against the stove.

Kian hands round brandies. Even to me.

"This might not be such a good idea," says Amalphia, twirling the little glass in her hands. "Remember last time? And I haven't had alcohol for months." She lays it down on the slate hearth.

"Or solid food, I bet," says Will coming in with a plate of mince pies. Amalphia and Will kiss, and then press their foreheads together. "And look at your tan!" he says, when he stands back from her a little. "Mine's totally faded away."

"Yes, Treadwell," says Justin, his arm around Faye. "We're the beach babes in this family; don't go thinking you can steal the title for yourself!"

"I'm sure Scotland will wipe it straight off," she says.

"And have ye noticed the Christmas tree, Phi?" asks Holly. "Faye and Anna spent all day yesterday at it!"

Anna's stood by our father now, leaning against him as he strokes her hair, neither of them looking at Amalphia, both looking sulky. Oh yeah, he's worked his special magic on his daughter. I can see it.

"It's the most beautiful tree I've ever seen," says Amalphia. She gets up to have a good look at all the baubles and stuff and touches a glittery little dancer.

"I got that one from the ballet school shop in London," says Anna, taking a small step away from Papa Zolotov.

"She's lovely," says Amalphia. "Like you."

"Still got your heart set on going there, to that school?" I ask Anna because personally I think it's a dumb idea and can have only one source.

"Well, how could she fail?" says Justin. "She's got her mother's beautiful face and her father's long legs: she's made for it!"

Anna whirls round. "I have my own face and legs!" she shouts and shoots from the room. We all hear her thundering up the stairs.

"I'll go after her," says her father.

"No," says her mother. "Let me." And she shoots from the room too.

I talk to Lexi. I stay through in the sitting room with him and the twins and Faye. Until we're all summoned through to the kitchen. For traditional Christmas Eve mushroom soup round the long table.

Amalphia does well. She tries to be chatty and friendly, but everything she says just makes my father look more grumpy.

She tells us about the film she's signed to do with Crispin in January and that he's been working on it simultaneously with the polyamory one. She's ousted another actress from the role; many scenes were already filmed, so Amalphia just has to do parts of them which means filming will be shorter than usual for her.

"More scandal, Treadwell?" jokes Justin.

My father's glance is sharp.

"Not really," says Amalphia. "The other actress still got paid. Crispin had some sort of big row with her about how she was representing his character. It's a body-swap story. I'm playing a new-agey, eco-conscious person and Crispin's a right-wing, pro-oil political commentator. I buy a spell from a magic shop to help the world, it gets spilled during an altercation between us at a protest, and Crispin happens to utter the right words, and bam!" We're all engrossed with this story. "We wake up inside each other's bodies, though I've been told not to word it like that to the media."

Most people at the large kitchen table laugh. One guess who doesn't? I want to hit him again. Like, really want to. My fists buzz with it.

"I've been doing ballet," Amalphia says, changing the subject. "And you'll never guess who with?"

There are various guesses: Colin, Madame, Peter…

"Your old friend, Aleks: Pasha." This information doesn't go down any better than the film story. My father sort of fake smiles and looks down into his soup. She goes on: "I would be a lot thinner if it weren't for him. He's a very difficult man to say no to."

Finally he speaks: "And what is this that you have not been saying no to?"

Really? He's accusing her of having an affair?

She fixes him with a Hollywood smile and says: "Lunch. Lots and lots of lunch."

"Oh good, Malph," says Will, trying to diffuse things. "I don't know how you can survive on all that green shite of Truelove's." He proceeds to tell everyone how he had a near death experience due to 'slow starvation by smoothie' when he was out visiting Amalphia at Crispin's house.

Holly's made a cake of many layers of chocolate, vanilla and cream. Amalphia stares at it all cute and big-eyed.

"Tell me you're not looking at it like it's poison, Treadwell," says Justin. "Gone all allergic to refined grains and sugar in California, have you?"

"Of course not," she says. "It's wonderful. Thank you, Holly!"

"Ach, quiney, I'm just glad you're hame. Noo, I'll cut you a big piece."

"Not too big..." she says.

"We're not used to catering for film-star diets and portions here," says Aleks. He may have been going for humorous, but it comes out as snide, so I go with that.

I thump my fists into the table. "Will you give her even the tiniest of breaks?"

"I was only—"

"No, it's fine," she says, her hand on my arm. "But I think I'm going to take my cake through to the sitting room. There's ballet on TV. Anna, you want to sit with me and watch?" Of course she does, who wouldn't? "You can come too, Punchy Puncherson," Amalphia whispers to me. "It's Christmas, so no fighting please. And there's some stuff I need to tell you: a message from Crispin." She stands, but then turns back to the table for the smallest of seconds. "The soup was delicious, Aleks, thank you."

She doesn't give him time to answer, and we're very quickly all cuddled together under the sofa blanket, Amalphia, Anna, and me, Amalphia in the middle. The room is warm and bright from the fire and the sunshine. She's telling me that Crispin wants to offer me an acting job when Will comes into the room.

"Room for a small one?" he asks, looking at the three of us snuggled under the blanket.

"You're calling yourself a small one?" she says, laughing but shuffling over to allow him access.

"It's better than what Truelove calls Alexander," he says.

"What?" I say at the same time Amalphia says: "Will!"

"What's he call me?" I ask, because really, what?

"Well, you see," she says, "he calls Aleks, 'Pretty'—"

"And me, 'Rough,'" interjects Will.

She nods. "So he's named you, Alexander, 'Prettier When Younger.' I'm sorry."

I find this totally hilarious, but 'older' has heard us speaking, some of it anyway. He's followed her through here, like he can't give her a moment's peace.

"Who is this 'pretty younger' person?" he asks of the nickname. "Not you, Malphia, you grow more beautiful with each year that passes."

Is he being sarcastic? Cruel to her in some way that I don't understand?

He goes on, looking at her all the while: "The whole world sees it, and still you do not believe. This only increases the beauty."

"You've lost me," she says, but he offers her no further explanation for his words; he just stands there as if frozen.

The rest of the day is okay. There's no more sniping that I can see. There's food, food, and more food. And games. And excitement with the little ones putting up their stockings. And now we're all going out to Midnight Mass at the local church, which is cool. We've been doing that since I first came here all those years ago.

As we're heading out the door, Will stops my father and tells him: "You stay home."

At first I think this is something totally awesome happening, like an argument between the two of them, but no. Will turns to Amalphia: "You too, Malph. Stay here. Sort it out. Fight it out. Whatever you have to do."

So they do. They don't argue. They glance at each other and back at Will. He smiles and closes the door over the two of them. And I don't like it one little bit.

24

I'M AWARE OF VARIOUS things: the feeling of being at home and safe and warm and comfortable, and some feelings that are the exact opposite of that. There's warmth from the stove which means someone lit it, probably either Will or my father, so they know I'm here, that I slept on the sofa after Midnight Mass. But that's okay. I stretch out my legs and turn over, snuggling deeper into the blankets and the woody, cakey, comforting scent of this house.

But I can't go back to sleep. Because of the other thing. The opposite thing. The scent of... badness. I once overheard Amalphia describe this smell as 'winding its way through the air and trying to strangle you.' And she was right. Simone's perfume is fighting with the other scents in the room and, unfortunately, evil wins. So I lie still. And wait for her to go away.

She doesn't go away. She speaks: "Amalphia!" she says as I hear footsteps on the wooden floor. "You look like some sort of exotic stick insect, just landed from warmer climes. Which, of course, you have!" Fake Mum laughs her fake laugh.

"Hi, Simone," replies Amalphia, who I think has just come in from outside. She's brought fresh air in with her, and it dilutes Simone's sickening perfume a bit. "Happy Christmas," she adds.

"Oh, it's so lovely to see you!" gushes Simone. "And so brave of you to come back after everything! How are you? We were so worried after your little meltdown. I mean, should we be hiding the sharp objects and eating our dinners with spoons?"

This makes me want to leap up and reach for a sharp object, but I don't. I continue to lie still, as if sleeping, as if invisible; maybe they'll say more that way. Maybe I'll learn things.

Simone's still laughing. And speaking. "And good for you doing a little bit of acting! That'll be so therapeutic for you. Help put the whole Aleks situation out of mind, not that he can be blamed, of course. He's got a type, and her sanity must have been appealing."

"I have no idea what you're talking about, Simone," says Amalphia.

"Oh, I take it you didn't watch the documentary? Of course not – maybe they don't have TV where you've been being looked after – but Aleks's project is doing very well, despite your attempt to derail it. Look, here he is with his girlfriend. These are stills from the programme. Here, take my phone and have a scroll through."

I don't know what she's talking about either, but Amalphia's not having any of it. "Speak to me like this again, and I will have you removed from my house," she says.

"I'm just concerned, Amalphia," lies Simone. "For your children too. I know what it's like to have a mentally incapacitated mother, remember."

"No, that would be me, Fake Mum, wouldn't it?" I say, sitting up from under my blanket, causing Simone to give a small scream. Though really, that should be me too, the screaming. Because the sight of Simone is a bit of a shock. Her hair is green. Actually green. Neon green. Shoulder length and straight and green. Is it meant to be like that? Or has she dyed it one too many times and suffered some major hair fail? "Going for the 'wicked witch' look?" I ask her.

"Well, really!" she says.

"Feel free to leave if you're offended," says Amalphia, and I love her for it.

"Why is she even here today?" I ask.

"Aleks invited me," Simone informs us.

"Really?" asks Amalphia.

"Of course," says Simone. "Him and I have always been much closer than you like to admit, Amalphia."

"Simone, you really need to stop—" says Amalphia, and then her face changes. She goes from strong and assertive to unsure, the second she sees – I turn my head to follow her wide-eyed gaze – my father.

"Merry Christmas, Aleks," she says, then turning and going to close the outside doors.

"Oh, have you two not seen each other today, then?" asks Simone, grinning widely under the green hair. I can't stop staring at it, the hair. I wonder if it glows in the dark.

"I slept late," explains Amalphia, but Simone still looks happy.

I get it. She thinks they didn't sleep together. Maybe they didn't? Maybe Will's plan to get them to reconcile didn't work. I hope it didn't. I don't like being on the same side as Simone in anything, though. I shudder. And then I watch in horror as the day progresses.

Simone treats Amalphia as if she's an invalid. "Let me take that for you," she says of a heavy dish. This from a woman who never helps anyone and can't even vacuum because the machine is 'too heavy.' When Amalphia has one glass of wine, Simone whispers, really loudly, to no one in particular: "Should she really be drinking?"

Ross arrives in time for lunch in his kilt and carrying whisky. Holly brings a chocolate trifle, and gifts that go under the tree for later.

I'm assessing everyone's words and gestures in the light of the weird stuff Simone said this morning. I don't think there was a documentary or that my father has a girlfriend, but then why is he looking at his phone so much? Is there someone else he would rather be with? She notices too. Amalphia. I see her face. I see her wonder the same things. I give her a hug, and she looks concerned again. About me this time. It's just for a second, like some sort of doubt. And I don't know what that's about. Him, it must still be him. It can't be me.

"Simone, I will pay you to stop," offers Justin as Simone pats Amalphia's arm for the hundredth time.

"Probably her plan all along," I say and Justin high fives me.

"Why are you even here?" my father asks Simone.

"Amalphia invited me," she says with a smile.

And she's caught out in her gate-crashing lies. And Ross takes her home.

Justin stands up and holds his glass high. "Now, I ask you all to fill your glasses for... my wedding!"

"Our wedding," says Kian as we all file through to the sitting room to watch the show about it.

It starts with the castle. Shot from above. Big surprise. Then we have Kian and Justin's faces big on the screen as the camera pans back to show them all dressed up for their big day; they're in ballet poses outside on the lawn, feet and hands stretched towards one another. They run round in a big circle, and we're suddenly inside the castle amid the preparations.

And I'm everywhere. I seem to have been constantly scowling. It's mortifying. There's a voiceover telling the tale of the 'bad boy of ballet' and my inheritance, blah, blah, blah. But that's not what's so terrible. It's my face. Wherever I am, whatever I'm doing, I'm frowning. Just like my father. Raising a snide eyebrow at the flowers. Looking cynically across at the 'massive erection' on the lawn... Justin's voice is made to sound echoey for those two words.

I'm not much better at the wedding itself. For a moment I am; I look quite happy and relaxed when I'm talking to Bubbles. And she looks lush. Totally beautiful and perfect and lovely. I hope she's watching. I want to text her, but then again I don't want to draw her attention to my scowling face. Pretty soon I'm shown yelling at Chantal.

She's given a moment outside the castle as she's leaving. "I won't be back," she says.

"Good," I say here in the now, and everyone laughs.

There's the stone circle, the meal, the 'sexy dance' that I didn't understand. I now learn it was something Justin and Amalphia choreographed when they were in college.

Cut to Madame, under her hat: "I loved that piece from the first moment I saw it," she says. "I always knew those two would go far."

Cut to Amalphia: "Madame banned us from performing or even practicing the 'sexy dance' when we were at college. She said it was obscene and that we'd be lucky to get jobs as bus conductors."

Thankfully there's no hint of the Gavin stuff. I don't think him and Sadie are shown at all. Justin maybe doesn't even know about what went on. I find myself not quite believing what went on myself as I think back. 'What have I become?' is too terrifying a question to contemplate, so I settle on: what was I thinking? Too much drink. Too many pills. That must have been it.

We see the bouquets being tossed and Amalphia catching one. We see the grooms leave. We see people dancing. There's Crispin Truelove and me drinking together.

Cut to Crispin: "That boy'll go far, mark my words."

And that's it.

"I liked the Madame bits," I tell Justin.

"Couldn't resist putting that in," he says, and then: "Your bits were good too, my dear. You're a natural on the screen."

———ele———

I see them, my father and Amalphia, later, as I'm putting my coat on to head back to the castle. They're in their bedroom with the door open, and he's giving her a sparkly wrapped-up gift. I'm frozen in the dark hall, mesmerised, invisible to them.

"Oh my goodness," she says as she opens the gift and discovers little nesting dolls, all sparkly too. "They're like treasure!"

"Yes. This," he says.

They look at each other, her up, him down, and I think this is the moment of reconciliation. I shiver. Then a small figure races past me.

"Can I sleep in the middle again?" says Anna as she runs across the room and jumps onto the bed.

I smile in the dark and tiptoe through the sitting room and out into the night.

25

The Cottage

Well, my dear, this has to be the loneliest Christmas I've ever spent. Even Simone is gone off to see you at Amalphia's, and therein lies the joy, the redeeming factor, for I know you are happy there, and I also know that I'll see you tonight.

This small house is quiet. There's a drip somewhere, but I can't discern where. It's dark. Sometimes I wonder whether it's my mind, my sight, that has darkened, but no; Scotland in winter was ever this way. You've experienced the childhood fun of it all with your new family: the snow, the log fires, the hot chocolate. So wholesome. I am conflicted while thinking about it. I feel bitter when I think of my own childhood. Life was never warm and loving in the castle. Not for me.

I am conflicted, too, about my decision to leave the place to you. Is it really doing you a goodness? Don't feel you have to keep it; sell it, enjoy the freedom that money brings if you wish. Don't let the dark suck you in; don't explore the place too carefully. It holds secrets and stories, from history and from my own mistakes. Leave them where they are to dwindle away to harmless nothings in time.

There is no conflict in my feelings for you, though. I have managed to light a small fire in the sitting room grate here in the cottage and have looked out sandwich things for tonight. You will be full, stuffed to the gunnels with chocolate cake if I know Amalphia. And I do.

I missed seeing your face this morning. I'd been excited for that Christmas morning magic; your presents are all looked out here, but it will be Christmas evening magic we share. I ordered chestnuts to roast over the fire, crackers to pull, chocolate coins for your stocking, and tangerines. This may all be dull and old fashioned compared to the delights you will have enjoyed today, but I hope they will give you a happy memory.

I have a Christmas memory of your father, in fact I have many, but the first is the only one I can find any good in. I hadn't known him that long; we'd only just started working together, and he was yet to see any improvement in his condition. His arthritis. You wouldn't know he had it now, would you? But back then, well, things were very different. He was sweet to me that year, our alliance still fresh and unsoured. He took me to a restaurant with red décor that he thought I'd like; the tablecloth was made of gauzy, shimmery red stuff. I did like it. Strange how such details spring straight to mind, so vivid, almost like a photograph. He berated me for eating only salad. I remember that quite clearly: "A woman as beautiful as you can eat what she wants, no?" He persuaded me to have a spoonful of Christmas pudding, and he fed it to me; vile stuff, steeped in brandy, they set fire to it at the table. He was different then. Younger, less care-worn, I suppose. Extraordinarily good looking. But weak, frail; he needed help opening doors some days. He needed me. It made me feel strong. Special. That all changed, of course; as he healed, he grew in arrogance, but I don't want to think about that today. It's comforting to remember his smiling charm, a little light in the darkness of my life, in the darkness of this day.

It is completely dark now: Simone is home and you are not. I watched her climb out of William's car and waited to see him help you out, but no, he just drove away again. I was so angry with her.

I shouted, called her a stupid girl. She laughed and went upstairs, calling back down that you are going to London with the Zolotovs and there's nothing I can do about it. The time until I see you is now measured in weeks.

But I have calmed. I know this is best for you, the companionship you have found in that family is a sacred thing, an experience I know nothing of: siblings to laugh and play and fight with. I am comforting myself with Amalphia's food, for really, what nonsense to try and stay thin now. It is divine. Would my life have been happier had I eaten more? Had I followed her happy example? I made a huge Christmas dinner for myself with the foods Simone brought home. Nice storage boxes. I imagine Amalphia packed this up herself and I feel a connection to her, as if she'd done it lovingly. Especially for me.

I can imagine a different life. If circumstances were not what they are, all of us together. I would put aside my past with Aleks, all his indifference to my work, out of love and respect for Amalphia. We would all sit round their fire and their table. She and I would laugh together at memories of an adjusted past, a bearable one where my sharp tongue was the only weapon I had used against her. I would forgo my diet to enjoy her food and tell her how wonderful it was, how wonderful she was. I imagined all this as I ate the turkey and gravy and stuffing. I found myself eating the trifle like a small child, with my hands, as if Amalphia was really the mother I never had, the fixer of all my problems, feeding my body and my soul all at once.

I am rambling, I worry I am sounding unbalanced. But it does feel as if something is being fixed through you and her. She will care for you as no one did for me. She will mother you, protect you, love you, as no one did for you. Before.

But for now, Happy Christmas, dear Alexander. You deserve it.

Amalphia has sent me over a slice of what I think must be a chocolate Yule log; it is decorated with a small piece of marzipan holly, snow dusted berries to boot. I am going to eat it beside the glowing orange fire, with a cake fork, a lady again, but one who enjoys cake.

Michelle xxx

26

"I DID THAT," SAYS Will, and I want to punch him in the face.

This is a first for me. I've never wanted to hit Will. In fact I've never been as angry with anyone as I am in this moment, at least not that I can remember. But this is too much. It's unbelievable.

I mean, he treated her like shit; Zolotov treated Amalphia like shit. His screw-up was monumental, so how can she be all over him like she is? There's been soppy smiles and kisses all through the festive meal at the village pub. I'm not the only person to be pissed off about it. Justin's commented several times about how they're not the newlyweds at the table.

It makes no difference. She tells him: "Newly wedded bliss is a state of mind," and slides her hand between my father's shirt buttons – why, I don't know – then I'm almost angry at her too, but not really

I know why this has happened. She had a totally crap mum. Been there, worn that hat twice over. We're fucked in the head, her and me; for all her being a famous actress, her self-esteem must be non-existent to put up with him.

I look away from them and down at my beer and say, "Yeah, how did you do that?" to Will like it's no big deal. Like her, I can act too.

He grins. "Shut them in a room together. Well, a house. Rest of us went out. Looks like they've sorted things out this time."

Beer regurgitates into my mouth. I swallow it back down and look over at her, trying to blur my father into me. It doesn't work – I'm not even sure I want it to – but her big dark eyes glance my way for a second before she looks back at him and listens attentively to some crap he's spouting as if he matters. And I know why it's all so much worse this time. Something's different tonight, and it's all down to him. It's his fault.

He's told her. I just know it. He's fucking told her what he thinks he knows about my feelings, my 'crush,' as he calls it. Her attitude to me hasn't changed in any outward way. She still smiles and hugs and laughs, but a new reservation is there to be sensed by anyone who knows her well. And I do. She's holding back a little, wondering a little, but he doesn't have her completely convinced. I'll just have to show her that he's a jealous, lying idiot. And after dinner, at the festive dance, I do just that.

The large events hall of the hotel is 'hoaching' as Holly would say, and does; I hear her from across the room. Ross is setting everything up for the band, the speakers making strange and squeaky echoing noises as he adjusts them on the small stage. Lexi is wired, edgy, nervous and excited; he's getting to do a song later. Amalphia's been wandering about admiring the decorations; it's all done as she likes with natural green stuff and sparkles, a great big tree, and the floor cleared ready for dancing. It's like a personalised trap set to lure her in. I sometimes think the pub would've gone out of business years ago if it weren't for her. People come here in droves hoping she'll turn up, and, of course, she often does. Everyone's watching her, but she doesn't seem to notice.

My plan to undo my father's story proves pretty easy. There's a large number of eager young women about; all I have to do is go and speak to them, be friendly, laugh a bit, smile.

Their side of the conversation is fairly standard: is Amalphia Treadwell really your mother? Oh. Is she all right now? That was just awful what the press did to her... Is it true that you own the castle now? Must be affa lonely up there all by yersel...

Bring it, girlies.

I see her looking over as I pick a bit of stray fir tree out of a girl's hair. I see her say something to him, and he turns his head to look too. One little cosy dance, and I'm golden again.

He's not fooled, but there's nothing he can do about Amalphia's opinion now. She's over at the bar speaking to Will when I waltz back into her space, a young woman she used to teach at my side. The conversation turns to 'the castle back then.' I tell them I've done it all up for Christmas and invite them all to visit, to come and see, to dance and play piano and party.

Then Bubbles is all of a sudden here. Right beside me. I feel panicked. Where did she come from? I didn't know she was here. And she's in a funny mood, a cross mood, all up in my face with: "I don't suppose there's the slightest chance you'd lower yourself to dance with me?"

"Hey," I say in surprise. When is Bubbles ever angry with me? Hardly ever. Only if I'm doing something really stupid. "Hey," I say again, holding her back by the shoulders to examine her. She's wearing some slinky black dress and she looks... well, really hot actually. "Look at you, all grown-up," I tell her.

"Look at you, all: not so much," she says, waving a hand up and down in front of me, full of attitude. Her curly hair bounces as she tosses her head.

I lower my voice so Amalphia and Will don't hear. "Have you been drinking?"

"No!" she replies, more offended than ever and turns to leave.

I go after her. "Dance with me, Bubbles. Tell me what's up?"

"You can't order me to dance with you," she snaps and weaves away from me through the crowd.

I'm completely intrigued and more than a little worried, so I follow her over to where she's just sat down by Ariel and Henry. I didn't know they were here either. We talk about the babies and Christmas while Bubbles sits and huffs. Too much already!

"Dance?" I ask, holding out my hand. "Please?"

She puts her hand in mine. She looks me in the eye. And we walk to the dance floor where there's a waltzy thing going on.

"Nice dress," I say.

"I've been home," she tells me. "I can't believe they're all still there, everybody so much the same, you know. My mum and Jasmine need to move out, or kick my father out." She's blinking, all filled up with the frustration of it. I get it now. I get it so much. And I hug her in to me, and we sway for a while. Her hair smells all coconutty and sweet.

"And then," she says, looking up at me. "I come here and see you flirting your way round the world."

I'm about to deny it – I mean, the world? – but what's the point? "Just trying to wind my dad up," I tell her.

She looks at me, maybe like, despairingly? "We're all going away on tour again," she tells me. "In January. Amalphia's going back to the States, even your dad and Will are going to be gone, working on their project."

I nod. I know all this.

"You won't do anything too stupid, will you?" she asks.

"Like what?"

"Getting into fights?" she says. "Taking too many painkillers? Mixing them with alcohol? Sitting around moping in your great big castle? Running around underground being weird? Thinking dark, twisted thoughts in dark, twisted places? Or setting fire to things?"

It smarts, this list, like someone's chucked something nasty in my face. "I didn't realise you had such a low opinion of me."

"I don't," she says simply. "But I'm going back home now, and I just wanted to... I don't know, make sure you're okay? And check that you don't want to rethink things and come with us? On the tour, I mean?"

"No," I say, wanting to say so much more, to explain that I can never ever do that. I've left the school, his school. I'm nothing to do with it anymore. And my father probably wouldn't let/want me there anyway. But I just say: "I can't."

Then she's hugging me and her hair's all in my face, tickling, doing its coconut thing, before she's off through the multitudes. Lots of guys turn their heads to watch her go by. What's with all these letches in here tonight? And what's with her? I return to the bar as Bubbles leaves with Ariel and Henry, and I order another beer.

27

IT ISN'T LONG BEFORE Amalphia joins me at the bar. I get a cheek kiss and a really long searching look as she reads, or tries to read, my face. I hope everything that should stay hidden is, in fact, hidden. She tells me she's taking both the younger girls with her to L.A. in the New Year.

"I think it will be good for them," she says. "They can lie by the pool and unwind, do different ballet, meet different people."

Different ballet, meaning different from what my father teaches them? I smile my approval. Talk returns to the castle and whether it's still wild party time in the place. It isn't. It really isn't.

"I hope it isn't too cold and lonely?" asks Amalphia. "You know you can stay at home anytime. Stay tonight if you like—"

"That's fine," Will says to her, "but you won't be there."

We both look at him in question.

"You're staying here at the hotel," he tells her. "It's all arranged, honeymoon-style. Roses and chocolates and champagne. You need it, babe, the two of you. You deserve it."

She seems to be both cross and happy about this, and is soon off dancing with my father again. But I don't get Will doing this; isn't he shooting himself in the foot? He grins when I ask him about it a few minutes later.

"No, not at all," he insists. "It's been like a huge hole in my life, this distance between them; they need some time being just

146

them. I think they're okay now; they've argued it out, they've made up, but a little extra romance won't hurt. Though..." He studies them closely as they dance. "I may have misjudged something." He looks at me, as if wondering how much to say and then seems to decide I'm old enough or whatever because he leans over in confidence. "I arranged a basket of adult stuff for them. There's parts of their relationship that I don't exactly get; they're a lot wilder than me in some ways. But they're looking all soft and sweet together tonight, don't you think?"

Yeah, I do think, and it's sick-making. One minute she's looking up at my father as if he's some sort of god, then her hands are behind his neck as she leans against him, holding him as if he's a precious thing. I grunt in agreement with Will.

"Crap," he says, looking worried. "It was a spur of the moment impulse. Maybe it was selfish. Letting them know I'm cool with it all, even though I don't do the hardcore stuff myself. And after everything that's happened, if the press should get wind of it... Fuck. Maybe it's not too late to stop it." And he's on his phone to Amalphia's assistant, but it seems the gift basket has already been delivered to the hotel.

It's the word 'hardcore' I can't get past as I stare at Zolotov through the throng. What does he do to her? Amalphia should be treated like a princess, not... and I have to know.

"What's in the basket?" I ask Will.

"I'm not exactly sure actually," he says. "I let the shop staff pick their best-selling stuff. I was so happy about them making up, I mean, look at them." I choose not to. "I got a bit carried away," he adds unnecessarily.

"So it's in her room now?" I ask. "Here in the hotel?"

He nods, forlorn.

"I'll get it back," I say. I have to; fuck knows what's in there. Whips? Chains? Things that'll encourage abuse of Amalphia. It's just not going to happen. I will do anything to stop it.

Bubbles has gone home and won't see my 'round the world' activities, so I get busy.

Gail McKay is a pretty girl, short dark hair, short dark dress, works in reception at the hotel and behind the bar sometimes. She's standing at the side of the hall girl-crushing on Amalphia like the rest of the room when I ask her to dance, a dance that soon gets hot and heavy and ends up out in the entrance lobby. "Can we get a room?" I ask her. "I mean, borrow one?"

She nods and laughs. So far, so good. We're soon through in the back office of the hotel where the room keys are kept. She takes a key with '2' emblazoned on it.

"Is '1' better?" I ask her. "Nothing but the best for you."

"No," she says, laughing. "That's the bosses' bedroom, and Amalphia's got '3' tonight, so this is your lot."

I kiss her against the wall and slip key number three off the hook and into my pocket while she's not looking. The rest is plain sailing. As soon as we go into our room, I pretend to get a text and exit, telling her I'll be back in a minute.

Will has had a proper job done on Amalphia's room. There's a line of heart-shaped chocolates strewn across the pillows and so many vases of roses that the place stinks like a florists. Or a castle done up for a wedding. That's what the smell reminds me of.

The basket of torture lies in the middle of the bed, all wrapped up with velvety stuff and ribbons. It's heavy.

Back in the dim hallway, I realise I can't just dump the thing somewhere; someone might find it, might put two and two together and link it back to Amalphia staying here tonight. No, I'll have to get it right out of here. I make my way out the back entrance of the hotel unseen, having known about this exit since I took Lexi through it to vomit once during a teen dance in the hall.

Now what? Taxi, that's what.

I'm back at the castle in less than ten minutes. It's so quiet. I close the heavy front door carefully but the sound still echoes all around the foyer. Angels stare down at me in judgement. It is cold in here; Amalphia was right about that.

I somehow don't want to take the elevator up to my room; I don't want to make any noise, despite the fact that it's just me here. Instead I walk the round-and-round trail up the stairs, even though it still makes my ankle twinge and ping, and then I lay the evil package on my current, her old, bed. It's like opening a demonic Christmas gift. I hold a tube of specialist anal lube. Condoms made for that purpose too. I'm shaking as I look through the rest. A gag, a blindfold, handcuffs, sensual oils, a slinky rope. At a stag do this would be a bit of hilarity, but that's not what's happening here, not what was supposed to be happening tonight.

He was going to use this stuff on her, use her for his own pleasure, like she's a doll, a toy, a thing. I squirt the lube – it's bright blue – down the toilet, like that can erase it from her life. I swallow two strong capsules from the medicine cabinet as I watch the blue stuff flush away. The rest of the 'gift' items, I take downstairs to the kitchen, tie them all up in a black plastic bag and carry it out to the bins round the back of the castle.

The moon is a thin crescent in the sky over the tall pine trees, and there's a nip of frost in the air. There's just enough moonlight to make out a silver shimmer on the top turrets near her room, my room, the top of the tower. These are the things she would notice, the things that would make her smile. Not that filth in the bin. And not him.

Ross left his bike here tonight. I take it back to the pub. I need to let her know I'm near, that I'm here for her whenever she needs me. One day she'll see. One day she'll be free.

28

I AM FEELING MONUMENTALLY pissed off as I sit on the stone in the pool. Quite a leap is needed to reach it now without getting wet but I've perfected the feat, or perhaps years of ballet have trained me for it. The trees are bare; they cut a dark and twiggy silhouette against the pale grey sky and cast a mirror-like reflection in the water. I text Bubbles a photo of the place; I think she'll be impressed with how much bigger the pool is now. I click through onto the school blog and watch the latest clips. Bubbles smiles up at me from the screen, and I calm down a bit.

A small black coot emerges from the reeds at the side of the pool and darts about, like it's searching for something, food I suppose. The surface of the water turns dark and murky in the bird's wake, the trees all mixed up and disordered. Like me. And I'm angry again.

Ross is right. That's what I'm angry about. That's what's so fucking annoying. I had a massive argument with him this morning, and I know really that all the rubbish he said to me isn't really rubbish. At some point I will have to do something to earn some money. I denied it at first, but it's true about the castle costing a bomb to maintain. So far this year there's been a plumber's bill for frozen pipes (I've got the heating on all over the place now to avoid that happening again, and that's going to cost more), the roofer's sent in his bill for the leak in the tower (I think I've been swindled there) and the insurance has tripled now they've learned that it's just me looking after the castle and not some responsible educational trust.

The cost of electricity is astronomical, and it seems to use itself even when there's nothing on. I deactivated all the fire and burglar alarms, because really, if the place hasn't been robbed or burned down already, when's that ever going to happen? We don't need to heat the swimming pool; Alexei and me are the only ones staying here now, and we don't use it anymore. So, some economies have been made.

Ross is right about the other thing too, though. Money aside, I do need something to do.

The pool is done, transformed into a proper 'lochan' once more, the 'Castle Loch.' It's beautiful. I feel I've achieved something here, made it better, made something Faye or Bubbles will want to swim in anyway.

I slip as I try to stand and end up thigh deep in the pool, feet sinking into the mush that is its bottom. The coot flies up, startled out of its dinner search, and I go in search of mine. There's still a chunk of Michelle's money left, after all, a huge chunk actually, and I've all the time in the world.

My sanctimonious cousin sits on his bike in front of the big old castle door thinking he looks cool in his retro biker jacket. Surely he can't have more to say? But no, it's more of a 'take back' that happens.

"I dinna' mean to be a prick," he tells me. "If you're interested in the history of the place, Michelle had a bunch of books and old letters, that type of thing. They'd keep you busy for a bit."

"Oh yeah," I say, putting extra sarcasm into my tone, because sometime he misses it. "Sounds fascinating."

"There's her research too, you ken. It wasn't all dance and science. She wrote lots of stuff, lots of papers. Maybe some of it could be published. She'd like that."

He always speaks about her as if she's still around, still here to like things, which is kind of annoying. But sad too, I suppose. And I don't want to hear it.

"Fitever," he says, putting on his helmet and adjusting the chin strap. "She stored a fair heap of it in that compartment under your bedroom floor. I caught sight of it once just before the rest of them came here. When the school was first starting up, ye ken? You should have the key in your collection. It'd be real small, not like a door one. She was right scunnert that Zolotov gave Amalphia that room, and she couldn't get into it anymore. She was going to try and get her computer out of there at Christmas, but Phi and him came back early then too. I remember that. She was fizzing. Something for you to fix for her now, maybe?"

Gravel hits my shins as he takes off over the drive, my drive, like way too fast, then swerves the bike over the grass, cutting a deep muddy curve across the lawn. My lawn. My grass.

"I'll have to pay to fix that, you know!" I yell after him, not that he can hear me over the roar of the bike.

I stand a moment, engulfed in petrol fumes, furious about the damage, then decide to not be that person, and turn and walk up the steps into the castle, jangling my keys in my pocket.

29

IT'S ONLY THE BEST fucking thing I've ever seen. Ever watched. Ever anything. It took me a while to work out the file and folder system on the ancient laptop, but I've got it now; it's all done by date and then by room.

Forget Michelle's dusty piles of old papers and books that I found under the floor. Though, while reading through some of it, I did find out that Ross is, in fact, NOT my cousin after all. Our families have some sort of old business link through the castle, and that's all. So he's not actually related to me. I know Holly's always going on about how it's not biology that makes a real family, but, I think, you know, that truth should come into it too. Somewhere. Surely. Everything's always so strange and hidden and twisted with us, the Manteiths. This cupboard of antiques and history that I've found in the bedroom floor is like a wooden example of the way we are.

Our strangeness should make the old pile of papers, some of them in such fancy handwriting that I can't read them, interesting. But nothing is interesting compared to the contents of the chunky laptop.

You can forget the old portrait I found down there too. I actually wish I could forget it. It gave me such a heart-stopping moment of shock, that painting, staring out from the back of the mysterious recess in the floor of my bedroom (like, who knew?), life-size and looking just like Amalphia. On closer in-

153

spection, it obviously wasn't her; it was some really ancient painting, reminding me of the one of the Mermaid and the Bear we were shown last year for the TV documentary. It looks like it's by the same artist. But it made me feel watched, that picture, like the real Amalphia knew I was sneaking around and up to no good. And now I really am up to no good, looking at all this stuff on the laptop.

I take a break from the computer – it's running so frustratingly slow anyway – and Lexi and I trek through the woods to put the heavy picture in Faye's room; it's the kind of thing she likes. We also leave the handwritten – I want to say, manuscript? – that I found. It's super old too. Says 'Isobell Manteith' near the top. It's properly historical anyway, so yeah, I leave that there too.

Once back in the castle, Lexi heads back up to the first floor to game on one of the big screens in the best upstairs studio, and I forget all about the historical stuff. It's more recent history that has me wanting more, like a soap opera or painkiller. Michelle's old computer was buried deep under the books and papers, but now that it's been unearthed, it fills my days.

There's four months of footage of my favourite people, and some of my least favourite, and it's just the best thing ever. To think it was here all the time and nobody knew. And only I know now.

The earliest video entry is located in the folder entitled 'foyer,' and it shows black for a few seconds before flickering to an angry-looking Michelle, a young Michelle, hands on hips, glaring at me like I've been very, very bad. I almost fall off the bed with the surprise of it. She never looked at me like that in real life, not ever. She was always just doting old Granny, the polar opposite of Simone, and always in some sort of baggy grey jersey. Here she's in a smart red jacket, and she's got a tonne of lipstick on her mouth. She's reaching forward to adjust something and then calling to someone over her shoulder.

"I should be the one up there, nae you," says not-my-cousin Ross, looking up at her and, as it feels, out of the screen at me too. He's really young as well. "But it's all working fine," he tells her.

"Good," she says, and with that, the clip ends and they're gone.

I'm more tentative about opening the next 'foyer' file in case someone is glaring out at me again. But they're not. I instantly recognise my father as he strides forward towards the main door, his back to me. The camera must be situated somewhere above the start of the stairs, I think. He goes out the door, and the film cuts off and then restarts with him coming back in. I get that the camera is motion activated. He comes towards me and disappears up the stairs. The pattern of camera off/camera on/Zolotov striding back and forth repeats three times. It's becoming a little boring. Then there's an altercation with red-skirt-suit Michelle that seems to be about the fact that he's smoking in the castle. The hypocrisy! I recall a lecture on the health hazards of nicotine from him when I was twelve, and Alexei and I had tried smoking to see what it was like. In the video, he goes out the door again, and I shut the lid.

Something weird is building up inside me as I watch this stuff. Him. And her. Together. Michelle and Aleks. Michelle Manteith. Aleksandr Zolotov. I never saw that in real life. They were never in the same room at once. Always separate, apart, secret. But obviously I know it happened. The two of them. I mean: I'm their kid.

My ankle hurts. The trek through the woods has made it worse. My head hurts. These films on the computer are making it worse too.

155

I take three little pills designed to help period pain – thank you, Amalphia's medicine cabinet – and now what? I hesitate as I put my fingers on the laptop keyboard. I could be about to find out everything I ever wanted to know. Everything that was kept from me. I could be about to find out way more than I want to know, way more than is comfortable. I mean, they didn't tell me stuff for a reason, right? I remember Bubbles saying something like that once, after we'd been down there in the deeper parts of the dungeon.

The pills are really kicking in now and starting to do some weird magic, so I think I'll manage to deal with whatever's coming. I have to deal. I have to know.

30

I LIE BACK ON my pillows and open the next file, and then it's all so fascinating that I forget any concerns about what's coming and just let myself be immersed in the past. The past of the castle. The past of my castle.

My father comes back into the foyer from outside. And everyone else is with him! There's nineteen-year-old Amalphia, eyes looking so huge in her slim face, as she stares about at everything. There's Will. And Justin. And Ruaridh, the photographer. Wow, even Sadie, of wedding/Gavin/weird-childhood-memories horror, is there. With Simone. My deranged sister is the only one not staring around in wonder. I'm guessing she's been here before, with Michelle.

I don't understand my father's reaction to the arrival, though. He was so excited and impatient beforehand, but he doesn't seem happy now they're all here. I wish I could hear what he's saying to Amalphia, but the sound equipment is obviously not that great. Justin joins in the conversation briefly before Zolotov directs everyone to the stairs and, with a sort of whoosh noise, they pass under me and away. Holly and some other guy head to the great hall, but my father just stands there, looking my way, looking up the stairs, I suppose.

He's really not happy. He's staring after them, her, and clenching his fists. Shouldn't he be all, 'Yay, I get to hit that piece of sweet ass tonight?' And then I feel as unhappy as he looks.

No one should think like that about Amalphia. And he clearly isn't. He's standing so still on the chessboard of a floor that it's as if the film has paused. Only the rhythmic tightening and loosening of his fists reveal that it's still playing. It's not enough for the motion sensors, though, and the scene soon clicks off.

I rewind back to look at her again because she's so different. This is Amalphia before she had kids, before she made films, before she was married to him. She's thin but not skinny like Simone. It's her wide-eyed innocence that gets me. He's older. He's her teacher. She's in a new country, a new school, so him being in a relationship with her is wrong on so many levels.

'The great hall' feed for the same day is a great disappointment. I see the tops of people's heads as they eat dinner and sit by the fire. No sound, no detail.

The next day's files are better; I think this is the way it's going to go, improving all the time, but I don't let myself look ahead. I don't want to miss a thing or spoil the story. 'Dungeon' and 'Pool' have been added to the feed list. The dungeon studio's a bit different with swords and all sorts of stuff on bare stone walls, not clean and white as it is now. Amalphia doesn't like it. I can tell. So can Michelle and Will. They speak to her. Zolotov doesn't care or notice, just plays the piano like the big show off he is. Only Simone seems impressed by him.

They do class and pas de deux down there. The sound is perfect in the large studio, the camera obviously having been placed at the front of the room. I can see every expression on every face, and there's a lot of bad feeling as they argue about dancing partners. My father's pissed off with Michelle, and Amalphia's pissed off with him. Simone's all over him. Will looks happy enough to be dancing with Amalphia, and I have to remind myself that this was before they were together. You can see how he cares for her, though. Even back then.

But she is with my father, right? They got together in London before this. I've heard the family stories about that. But, watching these videos, you'd think he was with Simone. The two of them sit and eat together, and they attend a weird-looking party together. Ross looks a right twat in his kilt at that event, but then he always does. He dances with Amalphia, looks to be teaching her Scottish country dancing. Weird grows again. Dear old Dad is joined at the hip with Sinister Sister who I'm pretty sure is wearing that same red dress she wears to everything, but it's difficult to make stuff out properly. The lighting is dim, and I can't hear anything anyone's saying. It's not till the third day of files that things really hot up.

It's like watching an exciting movie; I'm totally gripped. Amalphia's sent out of morning class in the dungeon, and I feel outraged on her behalf. What a bitch Michelle was in the way she spoke to her; I'm getting to see why Amalphia would've hated her. I quickly learn how to chase people through the different room feeds. Amalphia meets Holly in the foyer and heads across the great hall. But then she disappears for the rest of the day which is wholly frustrating for me, and for Papa Zolotov. He's wound tight.

And then in the days that follow: what a prick! The way he talks to her in class! I can tell he's still totally into her by the way he's staring at her when she talks, or moves, or does anything really, but he's being a right jerk.

She's angry. She's hurt. She turns to Will; they keep hugging and vanishing off through doors together. Why no cameras outside, why?

Simone seems to be getting with my dad from what I can see of the great hall view. But then there's a sudden change that I don't understand. He starts sitting with Michelle at the staff table during mealtimes instead of with Simone at the student table. I wonder if I'm about to be conceived.

Then I come to a bizarre class where he seems to be having some sort of breakdown. It's like he doesn't know how to teach anymore. Michelle's cross. Amalphia's worried. No, scratch that, Amalphia's sad. Did they break up? I feel celebratory as if it's a situation that can last on into the present day.

I watch Will and Amalphia rehearse a bit of *Romeo and Juliet*. Balcony scene, I think. They kiss during it, like really kiss. Zolotov the older is well fucked off. I'm not. I'm down with that, with their relationship. But he wasn't. Not from the start.

On it all goes. I begin to feel a bit bored. I mean, Amalphia and Will are amazing, but class is just boring old class after a while. Boring old ballet. Michelle's research stuff is the same every day too. I recognise the forbidden 'Amalgamation C' that she taught me. That freaked Amalphia out when she caught me doing it as a kid. Then, as I head on into the next day of data, I find a bunch of new feeds named for the students.

Bingo! I've got bedrooms.

31

WHAT A LET-DOWN. I thought these new feeds would be exciting, but they SO aren't. The view of Amalphia's bedroom is black, with the odd fuzzy noise. Not that I was going to letch on her. Or anyone for that matter. The cameras are properly creepy; I know that, and I'm not going to be creepy too.

The rest of the rooms aren't much better, because what would I want to see in them anyway? My father is hardly in his; there's a daily fetching of clothes, and I think he goes into the ensuite to shower sometimes. No guesses needed to work out where he's spending his nights.

Will's room has poor quality lighting and sound but when I realise I'm watching him masturbating under the covers I decide not to look there again. Some things you don't need to see, like ever.

Then there's Ruaridh and Sun – I've met them a few times over the years – they both read books a lot in their rooms. Simone prances around naked in hers. WTF? That was a scarring few seconds. So I just do a once-a-day check on Amalphia and my father in case anything interesting like an argument happens. It doesn't. At least, not in front of any camera.

The videos of the downstairs have become more interesting, though. I watch Amalphia do a beautiful dance in the dungeon: once through really technical, and then once – holy fuck – with so much emotion or 'heart' as my father is stressing to everyone.

Everything takes off from that moment because they're all rehearsing for a show, and I find myself wanting to learn every step along with them. But I'm stiff and sore, and my legs don't do as I want. Not just because of my ankle – take a nice big dose of medication, and I can ignore that – but because I've been sitting about so much.

So I do class with them. Every day. Back to the grind. And I enjoy it. Sure, it hurts. Sure, I have to modify for my injury. But it feels good. It's strange, but then, I have to admit, I always did enjoy ballet here: her happy classes, even his shouty ones; I liked the challenge then, and I do again now.

Lexi helps me set up the screen in the dungeon studio. I don't tell him about the laptop and what I've found on it. I think he's boring of staying here, and I don't want to creep him out and push him into leaving. It's better with him here.

We shift the collection of stuff I found in the outside pool to Faye's room at home so that, back in the castle, I can stand where Amalphia stands at the barre in the dungeon. My father's teaching feels different from how it is now. In some ways it's better, more inspired and spontaneous, but it's also a bit all over the place and not very well explained. I copy Amalphia and I'm fine. I hate to admit something else unfortunate, but she really gets him; she basically acted as translator of the exercises for the rest of her class back then, and she does for me in the here and now too.

I love her solo. I love the pas de deux she does with my dad and wish I had a partner to try it out with. I text Bubbles a still of it, on the off chance she might be up here. She likes the look of it, but she's still far away, in different theatres every week. Leading an exciting life without me.

Another upstairs studio appears in my file list, and I see the pas de trois with Justin and Will. Wow. Will was a choreographer back then too; it's experimental and intuitive and kind of inspiring.

It's all so awesome. I keep working along with them every day; my legs come back online and start to obey me again, but I'm nothing to her. She's better than I ever was. Why didn't she make a career of it? Could the companies she worked for not see her talent? Were they blind? They could have made a fortune out of her.

The weird turns up again when Michelle joins in with a musical thing. Seeing them working together, those women – Michelle, Simone, Sadie, Amalphia, and even Holly – it's a pure mind-fuck. I don't bother to learn any of that. Anyway, it's singing which I don't do, though I can see, or hear, that Amalphia is the only one of them who has any ability there.

When I get to the actual performance, I have to share it with someone; it's not something to sit watching alone on the hard dungeon floor. I transfer the file to my phone and project it onto the large screen in the theatre so Lexi can see too. He finds it hilarious which is a bit annoying.

"Oh no," he says of his mum and dad's pas de deux which, admittedly, is a stupidly sexed-up bit of choreography. My brother covers his eyes while it's on.

The guy who interrupted Justin's wedding is there in the audience, shouting out to Amalphia on stage. Zolotov looks pissed off. No one else allowed to pay her any attention then, Dad? He doesn't seem to pay her much himself at the dimly lit party that follows, but it's hard to see from my vantage point of: the ceiling.

Lexi gets bored and wanders away in this time and reality. I think he might be becoming addicted to gaming. Both him and me are spending all our time in front of screens now. He's left education and doesn't know what he wants to do yet. Part of me thinks maybe I should buy a car, like I said I would to Bubbles that time. We could go out then, see a bit of the world away from the castle.

But not today. My ankle throbs. I feel tired. I medicate myself and then turn my attention back to the laptop and its truly addictive little files.

After the show, in the past, everyone seems to go home for Christmas. The feed lists go dead. There's nothing for 'dungeon' or 'pool' or most bedrooms. Amalphia's is still listing something, but it shows the usual black nothing.

Then 'the great hall' has me covering my eyes like Lexi did earlier. Amalphia and my dad didn't go home and are enjoying sex in front of the fire. I'm glad it's blurry and far away. I don't want to see any, like, details of this stuff.

And that's basically all that happens in the next week of files. They eat by the fire too, sometimes naked, but by scar-preventing, dim firelight.

And then Michelle reappears from wherever she's been, and everything changes: a quick glance through the next few files shows harsh bright lights in the upstairs studios and harsh and bitter words from Michelle, and the weird grows in me again. What's going to happen next? Then. Now. I don't know. It's so confusing seeing my Real Mum like this. I get up. I walk away and take the elevator back up to the foyer.

I stand by the big fireplace in the great hall. Three trickles of water run down the white plaster wall and onto the mantelpiece, a situation that's obviously been ongoing for a while; dark trails have marked the wall. Something else in need of fixing. I watch as the water pools on the marble and then drips down onto the hearth. After a while, enough of it gathers there to seep onto the floorboards and into my socks. No roaring fire for me, no sex on the rug, no drinking hot chocolate while wrapped in a blanket, just wet feet and achy joints on the cold, cold floor.

32

I CAN'T STAY AWAY for long. The laptop calls me back, and I return to it, like an obedient little puppy or something. And at first, this next bit is intriguing. Fascinating even. Maybe it won't be so bad.

Amalphia, my father and Michelle. It's just them in the castle. Everybody else must still be on holiday. And it's weird. Super, super weird.

I watch the three of them up close and personal in the upstairs studio. Perfect sound, properly lit room, well placed camera. Michelle holds up a text book and talks about common thigh injuries. My father and Michelle agree on which muscles need strengthening to compensate for weakness and avoid a repeat injury, and then he suggests exercises.

They work it out on her. Amalphia. They hold her legs up and poke at her muscles. I'm not comfortable with it, and neither is she. She tells them they don't need her, and that she's going out for a walk.

"Enjoy the sun," he says, and then there's an extended kiss that leaves both women, and me, uncomfortable, which I think may have been the point.

Once Amalphia has untangled herself from my octopus-like father and left, Michelle turns to him, all serious and grave.

"You will be discreet about this, won't you, Aleks? It would look highly unprofessional in front of the new students. She's little more than a child herself, after all. In fact, isn't she still a teenager?"

"She is almost twenty," he says, stony faced. "And she is no child. She is very mature."

Michelle raises her eyebrows and fiddles with a gold chain at her neck. "Yes, her antics with Mr. Bevan certainly suggest maturity. But, seriously, you would risk your reputation for the sake of a fling?"

"It is not... This is not..." My father. Lost for words.

"Oh, come on! What are you saying? That you're going to marry her?" Her incredulity is intense, exaggerated to hurt and to mock.

"My private life is not your concern," he says in a clipped 'this is the end of the conversation' way.

"It's happening here around my work, so it is most definitely my concern. And I can offer you an objective view. I'm not accusing of you of anything abusive, Aleks, or, at least, the relationship is mutually exploitative. You're using her to boost your ego; she's using you to further her career."

"This is not what she is, not even a small part of this thing that you say is true." He's gone quite still, looking in the mirror rather than at her, and there's a hint of the fist-squeezing thing from that early scene in the foyer.

"You're taking me the wrong way," she insists, though he clearly isn't. And, in this, he's right. Amalphia is not a user. Michelle goes on: "Amalphia is an intelligent and talented young woman. I would say her future is quite well mapped out, wouldn't you? She's headed for a successful career in dance; and she's not going to have that if she spends her time popping out the next generation of Zolotovs for you, is she?"

His face twitches but he doesn't speak.

She continues. "William's in love with her; you must know that?" Her tone suggests she believes she is speaking to someone who barely knows anything. "Her affection for him is strong too; their patterns are constantly in tandem." She gestures towards the computer on the desk; it's just like this one that I'm watching now. "I have countless examples of that," she says. "And he's her contemporary. They'll work together, dance together; it'll all develop from there. But you could be right about her motivation. She's clever, so she must be aware that she's hardly hitching her wagon to a rising star by being with you. Maybe she pities you, Aleks?"

He steps forward and takes the text book from her.

"Okay, okay, back to work," she says with a smile, a mean smile.

He lifts the book up a little as if to say, 'Look at this.' He holds the middle of the spine and rips the thing in two, scattering the pages on the floor in front of her. He walks out. She rolls her eyes and follows.

I try to chase after them through the feeds but am frustrated by a lack of follow-on files. It's not till late afternoon that there's any action, and then it's only in the great hall.

My father walks in and sits alone at one of the long tables. I zoom in on the view which decreases the quality of the film, but I want to work this out; I want to understand all that's happening.

He jumps up and turns toward the kitchen, presumably having heard a noise. He sits back down again, turns away, and then there she is: Amaphia, entering from the kitchen passageway. I expect him to jump up and hold her, speak to her; surely he needs some reassurance after that conversation he had with Michelle? But he barely acknowledges her presence. She kneels on the bench beside him and places her hands on either side of his face. Always so intuitive, she knows something's wrong, and I wait for her to make it all better. For him. For me. I don't know. I'm feeling kinda weirded out again.

Michelle interrupts them, and I feel thoroughly pissed off at her. Are they to be given no peace at all? Possibly some of the 'him as me' habit is carrying into this; I'm taking it all really personally.

Amalphia sits back on the bench as Michelle lays down papers and books, and points at things in them. Amalphia is basically ignored. She asks something, they answer, she disappears into the kitchen only to return shortly with a tray of coffee and cake for them. She takes none for herself and exits.

I feel sort of desperate to find her. She crosses the foyer to the stairs. I find myself clicking through all the rooms in the tower, knowing that everyone is gone, so it's safe; there'll be no naked dancing to witness.

She's all alone in Will's room! Crying. Fucking sobbing her heart out on his bed. It's awful. I wipe at my own face with my sleeve and just watch her. I spend the whole evening wishing I could reach out and comfort her. I take the laptop down to that room, Will's old room. It smells really damp and is freezing, but I'm sitting in the same space that she was then. It makes me feel more connected to that time, maybe more to it than the time I'm living in. Which is seriously nuts but I don't care. I think I'm even sitting on the same bed as she was. It looks like the same one, anyway.

The day's files end with her going into Will's bathroom; the camera clicks off, then on again as she comes out. She's holding herself tall; you can't tell she's been crying. Amalphia the actress has appeared in time to go upstairs to her own room, upstairs to him.

The week continues in on a similar way. She's in Will's room a lot, not always crying, sometimes just lying on his bed reading a book, sometimes folding clothes. She's obviously avoiding my father and Michelle. She rarely has meals with them; I see her walk through the great hall and foyer with bits of toast and sandwiches and head to Will's room. Maybe this is going to be the start of the two of them being together? She must miss him a lot to be sitting in his room like this. I'm really hazy about exactly what order everything happened in their relationships, but I know that Will and her were a couple without my father for a while. I know that she left Zolotov at some point. And that must be when I came into being.

Thing is, my father and Michelle do not look like they're about to get up to anything sexy. I know no kids want to imagine their parents like that, but with these two, it's like: really? How could it happen? Like ever? I know they were together for a while before this, but now? Their conversation is stilted at best and almost exclusively about the work, except when she has a snipe at him.

"I'm only thinking about her, Aleks."

"You're only thinking about your work."

"And you? Are you even thinking at all? What about your condition—?"

"I am not stupid."

"No, you don't have that excuse. I do hope you won't interfere with the new teacher this term. It'll be good for Amalphia to have some space from you, to gain a better perspective maybe."

He picks up the now taped-together book. "Do you want to continue today?" he asks.

And with that they're back to ankle injuries and rotations. Huh. Maybe I should do some of those. But I don't.

Amalphia smiles from Will's bed, laughing at something on her phone; a text, a picture, a film, who knows? But I bet it's from Will.

33

I SIT IN MY bed and watch as Ross's face and dark hair fill the screen in this newly appeared room called 'D2.'

"I think that's it working," he says, drawing back a little from the camera. "But ye ken you're getting seriously scary noo?"

"You have no idea," replies Michelle from somewhere behind him.

"One computer not good enough for you, you have to have a whole wall of them?"

He sits down on a chair, and I see her. My mother, Real Mum, Michelle, is leaning against a rough stone wall. I recognise the big damp blocks of stone and the chains that hang from the wall on either side of Michelle as she stares at Ross. They're in the deeper part of the dungeon, where Bubbles and I filmed stuff last year, where Bubbles got trapped in the chains. Michelle is minus the jacket of her red skirt suit, and her hair is a bit all over the place. She looks different. She's all wide-eyed and flustered looking. It's unsettling and actually reminds me a bit of Bubbles when she was ill.

"It's my castle," she announces in what seems like way too loud a voice. "I can do what I like. You have to admit, it's impressive."

"Oh aye," he agrees, looking at something I can't see, beyond the scope of the camera.

"And this is a better control centre for me now," she says. "It's become so risky with so many more students going about this term. I'll come down here after hours."

"By yersel, like?" he asks with a wide smile.

She laughs and begins to unpin her messy hair. "I have a little job for you," she says. "Or I will have; let me work my magic first week of term, soften her up for you."

"You're nae on aboot Amalphia again?"

"You'd be good together," she says. "Bring her into the fold, the family; she's got the brain for it, you know."

What? I mean, what?

Ross frowns, possibly thinking the same as me. "I really dinna think—"

"I need to get her away from Aleks. He's twenty years older than her..." A smile forms on Michelle's face as she walks forward and places her hands on Ross's shoulders. "That's what I'll tell him tomorrow. In a relationship with such a big age difference as theirs, it'll always be the woman who attracts criticism. I'll say it could do her great harm. That'll get to him."

"I hope you never plot against me like this."

"Then don't give me need, bonny boy," she says with a laugh before hitching up her skirt and straddling him on the chair.

Oh no. Really? No.

"Do you have any other needs I should ken aboot?" he asks, and I slam the lid of the laptop shut. I suppose it's good that he's not really my cousin then. But... ugh.

I walk downstairs to what was my father's bedroom back then. Just down from mine now. Despite various people having stayed in this room over the years between then and now, there is still one clear sign that it was his. I saw it ages ago, and I search for it now. Right in the back of the towel cupboard, there's a small tub of super strong medication. Analgesic and anti-inflammatory. For arthritis. A long way past its use-by date. Just like this castle. This family. And me.

_ℓℓ_

New day. Both here and there. Now and then. New term there. New sick-making thing. Person. Whatever. Amalphia's new teacher is Colin McKen, a man I've met several times over the years. He was at Justin's wedding. That must have been another mistake with the guest list, like Sadie, surely? Will hates him, that's always been clear, and now I know why. The guy is a complete sleazeball, a harasser of women, especially Amalphia. Of course. As if it isn't bad enough that everyone I'm related to in this film is obsessing or plotting about her, he has to go and join in.

Everything he says is an innuendo. No, that's not quite right, it's less subtle than that; it's pure obscenity. I sit on the floor of the dungeon studio in open-mouthed horror rather than doing the exercises in this class, which are all rubbish anyway. He's such an ego on legs, probably doesn't think he has to even prepare to teach class. They're all horrified, everybody in the class. I wait for him to get his comeuppance, but it doesn't come. It all just gets worse.

My father is teaching the new students upstairs, and it's only Colin and Michelle that are downstairs in the morning. Mr. Timms still does pas de deux in the afternoons, but I have to watch McKen manhandle Amalphia through that as well; she's no longer partnering Will.

Day two of Sleazeball Ballet is really bad. McKen gets her to do everything en pointe, and when I say everything, I mean everything. She shakes her feet at the end of class; they must hurt like fuck. I rub my ankle in solidarity. Michelle decides this pointework thing is an excellent idea and adds in the notion that toe-protectors should not be used. I wait for Amalphia to refuse in no uncertain terms, but she just looks angry and gets on with it.

Day three she's depressed, slowed down, leaning on Will and Justin a bit, and by the fourth day of term, she's obviously ill. Why does no one tell her to stop, to lie down, to have a cup of tea even? The recent problem of her inability to look after herself and everyone else's inability to see it or help, is, well, not recent at all. My father and Michelle still work together upstairs on their therapeutic stuff after classes, but I hear no discussion of Amalphia's situation.

I'm getting quite instinctive about flicking between room files now. I have a quick look at my father's bedroom that night, and he's only bloody well in it. He's sat in the bed – by himself – reading a book. Did she tell him to fuck off? He doesn't look happy, but the camera soon abandons him; he's not moving about enough. Like me. I've stiffened up and got really cold and sore sitting here on the floor.

I join Lexi in the gaming chairs upstairs. I like that it's so different in this studio now, giving me a proper break from both the dark of the past and the current underground space. It actually feels like having a holiday or a break from something really nasty.

"Mum's been calling," my brother tells me. "Dad too. Will. Justin. They all say they can't get hold of you."

"No reception in the dungeon," I remind him, but I have actually been avoiding their texts and calls. I don't want to speak to the current-day versions of them. I need to finish up with the past first.

Lexi nods. "I lied to them and said we'd been going places. They're getting a bit intense about us being here all the time. Holly's filled the fridge again, and she told them you were nowhere to be seen when she was here."

"Let's order Chinese food," I suggest, perhaps in defiance of Holly and her tattle-telling ways.

Over the food, I tell him my car idea, and we agree that maybe we should get out of here sometimes. But then we just game. And game some more.

Blasting zombies is awesomely addictive. Shame I can't do the same to some of the people in that fucking laptop.

And I know I can't go out till I'm done with it. Till I've seen it through and know everything. So, much later that night, in my room at the top of the tower, I flex and squeeze my hands, like a warm-up, then I realise it looks a bit like Papa Zolotov's fist-squeezing thing and stop.

I open the old computer up, and get on with it.

34

DAY FIVE OF THIS terrible new term of the past. No Amalphia at breakfast or in class. Will and Justin are missing too. My father and Michelle sit happily and eat toast and grapefruit respectively. My father and Michelle teach and work happily upstairs and downstairs and all around. It's so frustrating. Does Amalphia not exist for them anymore? Have her injuries resulted in hospitalisation? Does anyone care?

And then I see her. During breakfast in the great hall, Ross hands her a motorcycle helmet and they exit the room together. I can't believe it. She fell for that? Didn't Justin and Will try to talk her out of it? They were sitting right there! The thought of Ross touching Amalphia suddenly becomes The Worst Thing.

I slam the lid shut and carry the laptop up to Will's room, then think better of it and head all the way up to my/her room. It's super cold in the castle now, and there's a heater in here. I need a hot shower and a lie down. Under the running water, I grow calmer and relax a bit.

No way. She wouldn't. She doesn't even like him. It's okay. It should be okay to go back and look.

I was right. She's back after lunch without Ross, but not before I see my father questioning Justin and Will, his stance telling me he feels just like me about the whole 'off out with Ross' thing.

Sunday is a day of no classes so nothing much to see.

Then Monday is good, so good. She's upstairs doing my father's class in her socks. The younger kids are completely in love with her, of course; who isn't? I study the two of them closely, and it seems like they're getting on better; something's different, though, like he's being very careful with her, properly gentle and considerate.

It doesn't last long, the gentle thing. Things soon get heated with Michelle. Down in the dungeon studio, Amalphia tells her to fuck off. This must be it, what Michelle was talking about in her letter. Amalphia's been injured due to Michelle and Colin's negligence, and now the two women are going to fight. For real. The things I've always wanted to know are about to be revealed.

I head down to the kitchen to make hot chocolate before watching. Before finding out. Before it all.

—— *ele* ——

This is going to be a night of pure entertainment, I just know it. This has to be the big showdown. I watch, fucking agog, as Amalphia tells him off, my father that is. She gives it to him good at the end of the day in the dungeon studio: he doesn't care what happens to them down there, she says; he's all happy upstairs in 'lipstick land.' She thinks he's with Michelle? That's so not right. Why doesn't he just tell her? He just says she doesn't know, doesn't have him all worked out, and then he kisses her. Given what's going on with them, it doesn't make sense, but she soon pushes him away. She complains about Colin and Michelle and then flies off the handle when he tells her she's going to have to get used to people looking at her.

I get her point. I love her for it. But I see his too, and it's confusing. He's not wrong. I'm looking at her. Now. Here. I feel my cheeks warm. Even eyes from the future are looking back at her. Weird, weird, go away. Come again another day.

I feel dizzy for a moment as I watch her run for the elevator. Escaping him but not me. Not quite yet. I chase her through the foyer. I find her in the great hall. Showdown! A big crowd gathers round as she talks to the top table, says angry stuff to the teachers.

Oh, for the love of proper sound equipment! Didn't it occur to Michelle that we might like to hear things from the great hall? What's the point of all the silent-film stuff?

And then I can't find them; Amalphia and her friends have gone from the hall and across the foyer, but they're nowhere to be seen.

Despondent, I start to flick though the bedroom feeds. Holy fuck, as Will would say. Papa Zolotov is sobbing on his bed, tearing at his hair, and shouting at the mirror in Ukrainian. I may be in too deep here. I don't like seeing this. All this time, he's seemed hard like stone to me, undeserving of her, and unfeeling. That I could handle. It's a relief when he disappears into the bathroom and the camera clicks off.

When it restarts, it's Amalphia's back that I'm looking at in the lamplight of his room. Bare feet. Big T-shirt. Bare legs. It's a bit weird. But then I'm transfixed, because there's no way anyone could look away from the scene that unfolds. Even though they should. They most definitely should.

He comes out of the bathroom and he's naked. Huh. Better endowed than me. And she hugs him, holds him. He shuts his eyes; he should be comforted, but it's like it hurts him. Doesn't stop him pulling off her T-shirt, though. Okay. My mother, naked. Stepmother, I remind myself. No biological relation. And then it's too much to watch. I don't want to watch, but I can't close the lid. It's like I'm frozen. In time. In the cold of the castle.

It's rough. They're wild together. I always thought he'd be, well, dull. Old-mannish. But I must be the one that's dull because I'm truly shocked.

And it just goes on and on. Different ways, different positions... I close my eyes for a bit, and then it's over and I wait to feel relieved. But what happens next is worse. For me, anyway.

They're so familiar, so close. Understanding each other without speaking. Just sitting there in the bed, drinking water. When they do start to talk, it seems like he's trying to fix stuff from before, saying the things he should have said then: how much he loves her, how he wants to spend his life with her. Turns out he's overheard some conversation I didn't; we're all spies here in this castle.

She thinks they're breaking up. She runs from the room, and I get a full frontal bouncing boob blast. I shut my eyes for a moment. I don't need to see that. He follows her, but they are not to be found. Upstairs, downstairs, all around. No files at all. I'm excluded now, and it is a genuine relief.

I find Michelle, though, underground, like it's just her and me together now. She's staring, close-up to a camera, or maybe it's just a basic webcam down there in the slimy dark of 'D2.' She's making scratches on the desk with a DIY style knife and smiling. Looking at things which should not be looked at. Spying. Plotting. Gazing from the corner.

It may be him that I look like, but I know now that the parent I take after is not my father. Definitely not my father.

I feel like I've had enough. I want to come away from all this, and return to the world of sunshine and beaches and family dinners. I wish I hadn't seen what I've seen tonight. But I've come so far. There's the big secret they've kept from me all these years. What really happened down there in 'D2.' The dungeon.

But it will be over soon. There's not many files left, so I'll do it all tonight and then be done with it.

And, on I go.

35

THEY REALLY MADE FURNITURE to last back in the olden times. Dragging this chair up these steps is possibly the hardest workout of my life. And I've been put through my paces by the great Aleksandr Zolotov. Not for a while, though. And it shows. I'm sweating, really sweating; I stop to wipe my eyes with my sleeve.

At least the lion heads of the chair arms are proper things to grab onto. And it's time to return the chair to its proper place. It's never been above ground in all the time I've known the castle, but surely it must have been once? Surely the great hall is where it belongs? I've got to make things right, you see.

You see. You see. Michelle said that a lot while she was talking, raving, whatever. I say it too, you see. I think it, you see. I should stop that. I suppose. You see.

I need to reset everything to a point where it worked, like you can do on an old computer, like Lexi advised me to do on that laptop when it froze once. I didn't do it, being too frightened of losing files. Well, it's happening to the castle now. A reset. A return to old times, before times. A complete do-over.

I pull the heavy wooden chair all the way through to the top table. I place it in the very centre of the top table. I don't judge this by eye. I get a tape measure from the cupboard in the passageway, the one that's full of tools and stuff that Ross uses when he's here. As Greeve. Greeve of the castle. For some reason this is suddenly very funny. The word 'Greeve.' Like grieve. And I sit on the floor and howl with the hilarity of it. I cling to a lion's head for support.

"Duce, have you totally lost it now? Should I call someone?"

"No, no." I stand up, trying to look sane, trying not to think about the word 'Greeve.' "I was just putting this chair back. It's the chair from down in the dungeon."

"Yeah?" Lexi looks suspicious. "I've never seen it before."

I open my mouth to tell him, no, not that dungeon, the other one, and to explain how I took Ross's welding machine and burnt away the seal to that particular dungeon this morning. But I don't. I shut my mouth. Lexi has never seen the rank hole, and it's best that he never does. Someone should stay innocent. I can protect my brother from the worst things.

"You hungry?" I ask him, and of course he is. He always is.

So I sit and eat a microwave burger right there in the exact middle of the table. On my throne, as Lexi calls it. He heats up some of Holly's soup and sits beside me to have it.

After lunch, my brother, my best friend in this whole empty world of mine, heads back to the house for a while, to get something, I think. To look for something? I can't remember. But I, the Manteith of the castle? I stay here. I have things to do.

_____ell_____

Michelle can talk. Really talk. On and on and on she goes from where she sits in the deeper dungeon. I sit at the top table and watch it all again. To make sure. You know, that I didn't just fall asleep last night and dream it all. That it wasn't just some giant nightmare. It was a nightmare, of course, but it was a real one, a living one.

Great big secrets that Michelle revealed during a soliloquy more horrifying than any from drama class or Shakespeare:

1. I was a test-tube baby. Planned well in advance. By one parent. One parent only.

2. So Papa Zolotov really didn't know anything about me. I always thought he probably did, and I always hated him for it. But the truth is that he genuinely couldn't understand how I could exist when I first came here. I was part of a plot, you see. A game. A castle game. Like Bubbles thought she was playing with the castle last year. I should find this last thought funny. Like, Greeve funny. But I don't. There's no funny left in me.

3. Simone is not only Michelle's daughter. Simone is also Michelle's sister. As in, they had the same father. So, I come from a long line of total bastards. Total sickos. That's my blood. That's me. I had to run to the toilet and vomit when I learned that. And then again for the next revelation.

4. I already knew that Simone was my sister. I've called her 'Fake Mum' since I found out that Michelle was my 'Real Mum.' But I didn't know that Simone gave birth to me, that she was the surrogate. At least that was the plan back then, so I assume it happened that way. I even remember Amalphia mentioning seeing Simone when she was pregnant, and I later assumed it had been some sort of fake pregnancy. But it wasn't. And how sick is that? And, I wonder, what does it all make me? I haven't worked that out yet. I don't even know what I'm meant to be working out anymore. It's all too fucked up and confusing.

5. And the great big secret that I wanted to know? I can't

really remember why I wanted to know it now. But it's this: when Michelle wrote in that letter about torturing Amalphia down in the dungeon? She really meant it. I mean, *really* meant it. Like in a physical way.

6. And, you see, she filmed it.

36

I'M THINKING ABOUT BUBBLES and the way her hair smells of coconut. I would like to stay thinking about her. About her smile, and how it feels when she looks at me. How I feel when she hugs me, and the things she said when I first saw her at Justin's wedding. She said I was sexy, like she really believed it. I would like to go back there, to that moment. Maybe make some different choices. Have a different sort of evening.

Now I'm thinking about how Bubbles and I kissed last summer. How that felt. Like nothing before. Like nothing else, ever. But I can't keep thinking about that. It's been a long time since that. I've done a lot of fucked-up things since then, and Bubbles is off doing her own thing, a long way away from me. Clinton and her have been partnering each other during the tour, and they look real cosy together. And then there's Aiden. She was real smitten with him last year, and they seemed to be reconnecting at the wedding.

But I don't go there. Can't have me dragging Aiden down into the dungeon and chaining him up. If I'm anything like Michelle. And I obviously am. Look what I did to that Gavin bloke.

My thoughts return to Bubbles herself. Serena as her actual beautiful name is. I wonder about her past. I know her grandfather was a paedo, a nonce. Like Michelle's father. My grandfather. I know Bubbles had an abortion when she was fourteen. I overheard that while listening at a door last year. Spying. Listening in secret. Like mother, like son. Bubbles deserves so much better than me. She deserves happiness. I hope she finds it.

I'm going to make hot chocolate. Lots and lots of hot chocolate. And I'm gonna sit here on my lion chair with my painkillers stacked up beside me. I can't go back to the dark places, the underground places, not even the dungeon studio, not ever again. I wear those places round my neck instead. Michelle's necklace is a map of the underground, after all, and it sits heavily against my heart. The tunnels and the dark and the caves and the chamber and 'D2,' the actual dungeon as it is, and, and... I don't know.

It's over for me, all that. And for the people in the laptop. I'm resetting them back to a time when they were happy, to when only good and loving things were going on here. From now on that's what's going to play in the theatre, just that one file, the sex film of them, Amalphia and Aleks, and nothing else. Perhaps it'll fix the castle. Perhaps it'll fix me. I'm not going to watch it – I'm not that big of a perv – but it'll play on here, erasing everything else.

Lexi is horrified when he comes back. He must hear the sound of the looped video as soon as he steps back into the castle – I've set it to maximum volume – because I see him head straight through to the theatre to investigate. Everything goes quiet. He must have switched the video off.

"That is my mum and dad!" he yells, coming into the great hall, seeing me sitting on my throne.

"Mine too," I tell him. "Mine too." I wish.

He doesn't stay. Which is good. Because he's too bright and golden for this place. He needs to go and live his life out there in the world. So he does. I hear the big front door bang as he leaves. And that's good and right. But what's he likely to do? Tell someone else, that's what.

I push my throne back and stand up. Because there is stuff to be done. And I sense that maybe I'd better get on with it or I might not get the chance.

There are great wrongs to be righted here in the castle. Evils to be purged. The biggest reset of all is going to happen now.

—*ell*—

The Cottage

Underground. Again. It's not good for me. So many things are not good for me. I am infuriated, aghast, with and at Simone. She has invited her 'old friend' Sadie to stay, purely with the motive of stirring the pot at the Zolotov's.

So I remain hidden. Scuttling about like a mouse in the basement unless they go out, and Sadie does go out. With Will.

"Why?" I demand.

"Why not?" my deranged daughter has the cheek to reply.

There was never any need to make trouble between Will and Amalphia; that was not the reason we came here. But I have given up the original cause too, and that rankles and annoys Simone. She will never have Aleks. She would never have won him anyway, but she is unable to see the truth of that. So she seeks to hurt and to maim where she can.

I no longer share that desire. I can't remember clearly why I ever wanted such things. Amalphia and Aleks and Will love each other. What's to disturb? Or to change?

But we're all vulnerable and needy in the end, at the end. I know I am. And I am alone. Completely alone. I would not wish this on another, not even one I have loathed in the past. Your father is what he is. He wasn't for me. I wasn't for him. Did I harbour hatred because of that? I don't know. Here at the end, I cannot see clearly as I once did.

Truth be told, the light is very poor down here so I can hardly see at all! There is a lantern with a candle. It's all very medieval. But it reminds and pulls. It drags me back to the dark and the pain and the horror. Low places. Dead places. Damp and dank. Screams and nightmares. I feel my mind waver and wobble.

Stay away from the dungeon, Alexander. Take the tunnel to the sea if you must go down there, but bypass that dark hole to the left. Shut it off. Bar the way. You stay in the light, my love. Burn bright. Set the world on fire with your dreams and your talent and your beauty!

Michelle xxx

37

Twelve long windows filling up with snow. Twelve long windows just about to go. There'll be no more long shapes of light cast across this floor when it's sunny. That's over now. I look up through the glass and watch the large white flakes swirl and circle their way down to the ground.

I walk outside into the snow. It's knee deep. I take one last look at the castle all lit up in the flood lights. I won't see it again after tonight. I'm almost ready. I'm almost done.

Back inside, I do a big walk around and put the lights on. All the lights on. Even cupboard lights. That seems right. Everything illuminated. No secrets left.

I'm going to walk the circle twelve times. That seems right for some reason. Amalphia always walks the circle, the stone circle, touching every stone as she passes. There are no stones here, of course, not in this great wooden pile of mine in this great, great hall of mine.

"Alexander!"

My name. My walk. My pyre.

I stand back and admire the pyre. I like the word pyre. Pyre, pyre, pyre. Rhymes with fire. There's a chair leg sticking out of it. The top table is at the bottom. It makes a good base. Holds everything else in position. I can see the benches that we all used to sit on. The kitchen table. The kitchen chopping boards. All wooden. All good. My pile. My mountain. My mother.

Her laptop sits on the very top. On my chair. My lion chair with its staring eyes. Should I climb up onto it too? It was really difficult to drag it up there... But I've lost count with my circles, so I have to start them again.

"Alexander." Amalphia's voice is quiet as she puts her hand on my arm. I look at the hand and the arm.

"You're got snow on you," I notice, looking at her. She's all dusted all over with it. It's in her hair and on her coat.

"Yes, sweetheart," she says, her eyes big as she studies my face. "You need to come home with me now."

Things. I remember things. "I am home," I tell her. "I'm here. You should go home. You are not safe here. I know what happened to you here."

"Alexei told me you'd found some old footage."

We stare at each other for a moment.

"I saw what happened in the dungeon," I explain. "The real dungeon."

She's nodding. Facing this. Facing me. "Michelle was psychotic at the time," she says. "She didn't remember any of it afterwards. It helped me, hearing that, knowing it hadn't been planned. We made our peace before she died, Alexander; I meant it when I told you that."

"You're not safe here," I repeat. "I'm like she was. So you need to go."

"You would never hurt me," she says like she believes it.

I walk away from her. I start the circles again. She follows. I turn and look her straight in the eye. "It's what I was made for. To hurt you. And him. Did you know that?"

"I know Michelle was sometimes unbalanced," she says. "We all have times of unbalance. You helped me when I was unwell last year. Let me help you now."

"I'm sicker than you know." I remember a bit of film from the laptop and quote it: "'Always you vill attract attention from men. Is something you will have to get used to.'"

That gets her. My perfect imitation of her husband. She steps back from me. She's thinking, thinking, thinking. I see it in her face.

"But you didn't learn, did you?" I say. "I was in love with you. All those years, and you didn't see. Maybe that was all part of the plan too."

"Alexander," she says, all deep and serious. "You had a boyish crush. It's a natural part of childhood."

"There's nothing natural about me."

She shakes her head. "Aleks had a similar infatuation when he was young, after he lost his parents. You had such a rough start in life—"

"It's why I said you weren't my mother," I interrupt. "To people. To you. As if that could make it okay."

"Alexander," she says, sounding all firm and teachery. "It's completely understandable that you would develop confused feelings for the first woman who showed you affection."

That's wrong. And she should face this truth now, I think. Because this is a moment of blatant truth before the end of everything. "Michelle showed me affection," I say. "She was always nice to me."

"Of course," she says. "She loved you very much, Alexander. You saved her, in many ways, I think."

I laugh. Me? Save someone? "I'm just a thing that was created to harm." A weapon. A sword forged to hurt and kill. "I'm hurting you now. I can see it."

She doesn't deny it. Any of it. Doesn't even try.

"Let's get a cup of tea," she says. "Or a hot chocolate; I know there's some in the kitchen cupboard." She takes my hand and I feel like I'm eight again. In her house. For the first time. Being comforted and cared for. For the first time. Because, though Michelle was nice to me, I don't think she knew how to look after a kid. So, I go with Amalphia now, a good little child doing what he's told.

We walk down the passageway to the kitchen. She puts the kettle on. Like everything's normal. Back how it used to be, even.

But it isn't normal. Of course it isn't. Her being here is actually super annoying. I was busy. I have things to do. So I have to get her out of here. For her own good and mine.

"She's down in the dungeon," I tell her.

"Who?" she asks, confused.

I really want to say Michelle. But that won't work. I know that. "Simone," I say instead and then quickly make up what I think is a totally believable story: "I dragged her through the glass floor," I say. "And then I tied her up in 'D2.' The dungeon. In the chains."

She looks at me in horror for a moment before speaking to me like I'm eight again.

"You're going to sit here at—" Her eyes take in the bare room. "You're going to stand here under the old fireplace arch and keep an eye on the kettle for me. I'll just be a minute."

I stare at the kettle. I stand still while she walks out of the room.

Then I follow.

The passageway is empty. She's moved fast. I walk.

I find her kneeling by the open glass door in that room, the one I tied Gavin up in. Or taped him up, I suppose. I used tape. I stay quiet and still now, hoping she won't look round and see me. I stay in the passageway by the door. I don't want to push her through that hole in the floor, but if I have to, I'll do it to keep her safe.

"Simone!" she shouts, but gets no answer. Well, duh. "Fuck," she says, and I like it. Amalphia almost never swears. Not in front of us kids, anyway. And then she does exactly what I need her to do. She turns and climbs down the wooden stairs that lead underground. She looks up at the little stone angel on the wall: "Yes, here I go again," she says to it. "Wish me luck."

She doesn't need luck. She's out of here. She can run down the sea tunnels and escape. But I suppose it's lucky that she doesn't see me here in the doorway. She doesn't see me walk across the room and shut and lock the glass door behind her either.

She must have heard it happen, though. I hear her banging on the glass and shouting as I walk away. I let the main door of the room swing shut too. And I go back to my work.

ell

It's beautiful. Like fireworks nights when we ate baked tatties and sausages that had been partly burnt in the fire. I remember happy faces in the orange glow.

I lie on the floor and gaze up at the roof of the great hall as the wood begins to blacken and bubble. It was too hard to climb up onto the pile in the end. I was knocking stuff down all over the place as I poured Ross's lawnmower fuel over everything. Plus, it's all smoky up there by the ceiling, but clearer down here. It's warm. It's comfy. I could go to sleep and never hurt anyone again.

But he comes. My father. It's so annoying. Why are my family determined to interrupt me today? Can't they see that I'm busy? He tells me that I'm his son and that he loves me and that we've got to go, and I tell him that I can't go because I've got things to do.

I stand to get rid of him, to fight him if I have to. One of the windows explodes. It's loud. Glass sparkles in the air. Like snowflakes.

"Come on," he says.

"I'm staying here," I say again, taking a step closer to the burning pyre.

And then – it's kinda great – he does the thing I've wanted him to do in, like forever. He punches me in the face.

—————

Blackness. Everything is blackness. Then I see my mum and dad. There's colours too and a roaring noise. I can't move. There's cold on one side of me and heat on the other. I manage to turn my head to see the source of the heat. The castle. On fire. It's not just the great hall now. The flames have spread. They're coming out the windows, reaching upwards, crawling up the walls like huge snakes or dragons. Destroying what was. Destroying what will be. Changing everything.

And a little way in front of me: there's my mum and dad. They really are my mum and my dad. I can see them properly now as if I've just woken up from a very long sleep, a lifelong sleep.

She's crying. She's holding him. She's shouting at him. "Don't leave me. Don't you dare leave me!" But he's out cold, lying on the ground, a fist over his chest. Then she's kissing his face, telling him she loves him, and sirens start to sound.

I still can't move. Breathing hurts. But I can't look away as the paramedic searches for a pulse in my dad's neck and doesn't find one.

My mum and dad, my Papa. They can't be broken because I've only just found them, only just recognised them for who they are. Don't leave me!

The castle is just one giant bonfire now. The great hall is a box of fire, the blaze from it reaching for the sky. It's deafeningly loud like it's screaming, shouting. Searing. Burn, burn, burn.

It's scorching my face and my eyes just being near it. I can hardly breathe with the smoke, but I can't look away. From them. From it. Everything is being burned to the ground now. Everything is being changed. Is this the great big do-over I wanted? No. And maybe, yes. Parts of it are.

The light is bright, and the medical mask thing hurts, and I'm going, going, gone. I'm lifted up, and Amalphia and my dad are in the distance now, fading away and, like me, gone.

38

I still can't speak. I know it's been a while, and people are worried. Doctors. Nurses. Amalphia.

I can't look at her. I know what I've done to her. To him. It builds up in my head, a swollen ball of poison and pain that just won't burst.

I remember things. The smell of the fuel as I sloshed it up the walls and over the pyre. It got on me too. I shouldn't be alive; but he saved me before he died, my dad did.

I remember trying to run away, and the nurse's voice: "We need help for Alexander!" Two other nurses, two guys, stopped me; they took me back to my room.

So I'm mad. Bat-shit crazy. Just like Michelle.

Calmness comes after a bit. I may be mad, but I'm not stupid; I know the calm is because I've been dosed with something, but it's okay. Reality is too much. My reality, anyway. The source of me. Created to separate and destroy. Nice work, Alexander. Job well done. Granny Michelle would be so pleased. Granny Michelle would be proud.

Not Granny. Mother. Flashes of what she did come too, the worst things I saw on the laptop; drugs don't block that out. I don't want to think about the dungeon or the spying or the blood – so much blood – but they are my ghosts, these things, these visions. They are my past. They're what I came from.

I don't want to see kind faces, so I stop looking at anyone. I don't want to hear kind words, so I cover my ears when any member of my family is here. They soon stop speaking and go. Will. Holly. The twins. Amalphia doesn't come anymore anyway.

Ross blabbers a bunch of stuff before I cover my ears: he says he shouldn't have told me about the secret compartment in the floor, but that he didn't know the computer was there. It's all about his own guilt, and I don't want to hear it.

Some things are very clear here in the new awareness of what's real and what's true. Lexi tries to hug me. I flinch away from him and curl up in a ball on the bed. A boy born of love shouldn't have to touch one born of evil. I know what I've done to him. To them all.

But when she finally comes, it's different. I wake up one afternoon to see Bubbles sitting on my hospital chair reading a comic. She glances at me and must see that I'm awake now, but she makes no effort to speak and just looks back at her comic. It seems wrong, cheeky somehow, and I want to call her out on it.

"Hey," is out of my mouth before I remember that I don't speak now.

"Hey," she says, not looking up from her reading. "Nice place you got here. Better than the room I was in."

I think that's why it's different. She knows.

"But then," she says, looking up at me, a glint of naughtiness in her eyes, "I was only involved in setting fire to part of a forest. You burnt down a whole castle."

"Is it completely burnt down?" I ask, suddenly interested. It is, after all, the easier of the subjects we could be talking about, the lesser of what I destroyed.

"Totally."

She comes forward and offers me a sweet from a paper bag, a chocolate. It's strange, like she's showing me a bag of life going on after all this. And I'm not ready for that.

"It's a smouldering ruin," she tells me. "Builders are there, making it safe. Amalphia's actually glad it's gone. She says she always hated the place, and that this is an improvement, a clearing away of bad energy. You know how she talks sometimes."

I do.

"Are you having a bad moment?" Bubbles asks. "Should I get someone? Will's just outside."

I don't want her to go, and yet, I do want her to go. Because I can't stop sobbing, and I don't want her to see. She sits on the bed and holds my head against her shoulder. She kisses me on the forehead; it feels like a blessing. And I cry. Like a baby, like the little child I was never allowed to be. Until someone else comes. A nurse. And Bubbles goes. And the calmness grows.

—ell—

Then there's so much talking. And, actual, literal, basket weaving and therapeutic art.

The people I see and talk to: Bubbles, Will, Lexi, Holly, Ross, nurses, cleaners, the psychiatrist.

I can feel the people I don't see, though. My father's all around me now he's gone. And I really think about him. How must it have been for him to learn about my existence? I can imagine I'm him – I mean, I've been practising that for years – in a relationship, a happy marriage, and then a kid from the past that you never knew about shows up with someone you never even slept with? And it might destroy your marriage. But it didn't.

Then he found out that Michelle was my mother after all she did to Amalphia. I wish I didn't know about that, wish I hadn't

197

seen. I would like the accident story back. I get why they told that lie now. But they came through that. Amalphia survived that. They kept it from us, the next generation, but they carried it with them every day. And I'm the kid who came out of it all. Not sure I would even have let me in the house. But they did. He did.

Will brings me a new phone – my old one must have melted in the castle – and the first thing I do with it is watch old clips of my father dancing. He's the better part of where I came from. At least I look like him. I could try harder to be like him. I know now that he was fucking amazing, even towards me, and now it's too late to make it up to him, to build any sort of relationship.

I can do other things, though. I stand at the window and look out at the grey city, its various spires in the distance. I assume first position, hands on the window sill. Demi plié. Tendu. Repeat. Doesn't hurt that much. My ankle is more-or-less okay. I was self-medicating other hurts. Using the injury as an excuse. Been talking about that with the doctors. I remember begging for painkillers when I first came here and them giving me other things instead. Things that I'm still on. I remember sweating and crying and screaming about it. But these memories don't really bother me; they don't embarrass me. Burning down a castle and killing your father puts these things in perspective, you know?

Once my muscles are warm, I do his exercises for injured ankles. The ones I saw him working out with Michelle on the laptop. I mean, I don't want to think about any of that. But some parts were good. I have to hold onto those, let them live. It's healthy. So say the doctors. And Bubbles. She gets right up and does the exercises with me. She hurt her shoulder on the tour. And I've got exercises for that too. And they help her. And I love that.

"I wish I could see him," I tell her. "You know, speak to him."

"You mean your father?"

I nod.

"Well, you should ask Will to take you. I'm sure it could be arranged. I can come, if you like?"

But I don't really want her to see me melt down again, so I say it's something I have to do on my own. She doesn't mind. She gets it. She sends Will in on her way out. And he's all for it. So here we go.

39

THE VISIT IS ALL arranged. I'm deemed safe to leave the ward for a couple of hours. With Will. As we drive, I tell him I've been watching old ballet footage of my dad.

"Amazing, wasn't he?" says Will.

"Yeah," I say, because he absolutely was.

I don't know where it actually is we're going, probably somewhere near home. Maybe the local graveyard by the church. I find myself retreating back into silence, and Will doesn't try to interrupt that.

Turns out, we're not going that far at all. We're pulling into a carpark in Aberdeen. The carpark of another hospital.

"Why are we here?" I ask. "I mean, is this where he is?"

"Oh, yeah, sorry, I should have said," explains Will as we walk through the wide and shiny entrance lobby, past places selling coffee and magazines and chocolate. "They haven't let him go yet; be a while, I think."

So. Post mortems and stuff are still going on. I'm not going to see his grave. I'm going to see his body.

I brace myself as we get into the elevator. Squeeze my fists. But maybe this is good. Maybe it's better. I can look at him and speak to him. Explain. And say sorry.

As we walk, I look at the overhead hanging signs, waiting to see them point the way to, what exactly? Mortuary? Morgue? Chapel of Rest? But they're all just: 'Ward this' and 'Ward that.'

I don't know how this all works and just follow Will, not really listening to what he's saying.

"Oh," he whispers as he stops in a doorway long before we've reached anywhere dark and deathly.

We do seem to be on a ward. It reminds me of where Amalphia was when she was pregnant with Anna and they made her go into hospital to rest for a bit. Will gestures for me to look into the room. I peek my head round the doorway and freeze. My father and Amalphia are in a bed; his arm is over her.

At first I think: she is way sicker than me even. But then: his fingers move as if to hold on to her more tightly.

Will continues in his loud whisper: "It's the only way either of them gets proper sleep just now; we'll go get a coffee and come back."

But I can't move. I can't look away. It's too good to be real. Here they are, still together after everything.

"Alive?" I eventually manage to whisper. "He's alive?"

"Well, yeah, of course he's—" Will pulls me back into the corridor. "Fuck, no. Tell me this isn't right? You didn't think—?"

I just look at him. I'm shaking.

Will is clearly horrified. "Dude. Alexander. Man, have we got to talk."

And so we do. Or he does, in the bright and noisy downstairs café over something pretending to be hot chocolate. The drink is nothing like they would make it, both of them, either of them.

I listen. And I learn. My father had a heart attack. He's since had two operations to correct an underlying problem with a heart valve that nobody knew about.

"Because he saved me," I say. "That's what caused it. That's what almost killed him." Almost; sometimes that's a big thing, a big difference, isn't it?

Will shakes his head. "No, mate. It was good it happened when he was around people. His heart was a ticking time-bomb."

"But I really fucked up." He has to give me that. I can't be let off with everything.

And he doesn't deny it. He just says: "We all do that sometimes."

"I burnt down the castle."

"I've done worse in my time."

I don't need to say anything. I just look at him, because: liar.

"You want the worst thing I've ever done?" he asks and I nod. "Cheated on Malph."

This feels unbelievable. "When?" I ask.

"When we were younger – it was just her and me back then – and she was struggling with her feelings for Aleks. And that's what I did to her. You want more? I almost slept with Simone once. That first year at the castle. Please tell me you haven't watched anything like that?"

"No," I choke out, more horrified that everyone knows what a creepy stalker I am than by his revelations. "I didn't see everything, mainly the classes."

"But you saw the dungeon, and what happened down there?"

Trust Will to be so straight like this, so direct. I don't need to reply; he sees my face.

"If you want to talk about any of it, that's fine. No more secrets in the Zolotov family. Malph's new rules. She is going to be fucking furious about this, though, about you thinking... what you were thinking."

I shake my head. "She's done with me, I know that."

"No. Why would you think that? Your doctor told her it was upsetting you, her visiting; told her to wait until you asked to see her. She'll be made up that you're here. She's so angry with

Aleks, it's cute. He's been having chest pains for months and not told anyone. She's livid. But she can't get mad at him while he's in recovery. So I'm bearing the brunt of it; we've got a hotel room nearby. I'm having to be more hardcore than I've ever—Fuck, sorry."

He's seen my face again. I feel my cheeks grow hot. "It's because she's my mother," I tell him. "I don't like her spoken about that way. I didn't really get that before. I didn't understand my own feelings. I told her some screwed-up stuff, in the castle that night, and then I locked her down there, down by the dungeon. I need to explain to her, to say sorry for it all."

"You'll get to; don't worry."

And then I want to explain to him too. "When I opened my eyes and saw them, on the ground, in the snow, it was like: oh, it's my mum and dad. I never really felt it before, but that's the truth. That's who they are to me."

"Let's go and see 'em then."

40

WILL GOES FIRST, INTO the room, and Amalphia is on him in a second, grabbing him by the shirt as if she's going to shake him.

"How is he? Tell me—" Then she sees me, and it's such a relief that there's only delight and love there. "Alexander." The hug is fierce, crushing, and then she's looking at me, like looking right into me to see what's what.

Him as well. My father. He gets off the bed and stands and looks at me. I walk over to him. Our hug is looser, but not guarded, not fake how things used to be. Everything's very real now.

"Thank you," I say to him. "Thank you for saving my life."

Will butts in before things get any more awkward. "Yeah," he says. "Alexander actually thought you were dead. You know, until today—"

"What?!" Amalphia shrieks. Will was right about how angry she is; fury is waiting there under the surface, ready to ignite. Her next words come out super carefully, as if she's forcing herself not to explode. "How is that possible?"

My dad sits down on the bed and gestures that I should too. He looks older, but maybe that's just because he's not been well. I take his advice and sit beside him while Will and Amalphia battle it out.

"I don't know," Will tells her. "We didn't want to say anything to upset him, so we decided not to mention the operations. None of us had any idea that you would have thought what you did, mate," he says to me, in a 'plea for help' tone.

"Bubbles did say something about you," I say, looking at my father. "About how you would be glad that I was getting better, but I didn't realise she meant—"

He lays his hand on my arm. "I am glad, very glad."

Amalphia sits down in the low padded hospital chair in front of us. "There's been far too much of this 'not wanting to upset people' thing going on in this family," she says. "We need to get to a point where we can speak about anything. No more secrets. Oh, I'm not blaming you, Alexander. Mental health problems can be difficult to identify for the sufferer, unlike chest pains."

"Malphia, I thought it was stress."

"Don't start. You have chest pains? You see a doctor. End of. But I don't just mean this. I mean all of it. We should never have lied to our children about what happened in the dungeon." I know she's eyeing me, maybe trying to judge if it's the right time to go on, if I'm strong enough. "We've put that right. We've told them, not details, but the basic facts."

"Did you know how Michelle made me?" I ask because I have to. "And why?"

"Yes," Amalphia answers at once. "She told me the day she died. But she also told me how she'd come to love you and how she no longer wished any of us harm. I told her that you were the good she had done, how she was leaving the world a better place because it had you in it." She looks to the side as if remembering. "But that knowledge of how you came to be... That must have been a terrible moment for you, Alexander."

"Yeah," I admit. "I watched a film of her, Michelle, raving in the dungeon, going on and on. And then it felt like I was just like her. Watching the camera feeds. Spying. Plotting." I look down. This bit is harder than anticipated even. "Having inappropriate feelings for people."

She's back to gentle, and it's not a question when she says: "Me."

"You. My mother, yeah." And so I tell it again, all about my waking-up moment, seeing them for who they were. They believe me, or they seem to.

"Nobody has more reason to have mother issues," my father points out, and the conversation moves on to easier things.

I visit them every day after that. I speak to them all, all my family, sometimes individually and sometimes all together. And things get better. Everything eases. There's still this amazing clarity, though. I look at them, my three parents, and see them for who and what they are in this moment, previous projections removed. Yeah, there's been a lot of 'psychological talk' with the psychiatrist, but this is just so true.

I can see that they're terrified. Terrified of Aleks dying, terrified of losing each other, of being apart if he dies. They don't say it, but it's all mixed in with their concern for me, behind their smiles and in their tenderness to one another. Amalphia's words sometimes belie the fact, but her love is there in her strictness, and her criticism of my father; it's ferocious and huge. It's overwhelming sometimes. But no one minds if I'm quiet for a bit, if I just sit and observe.

And I know that I want that. I want to find a love like that. I feel the possibilities of life again, or maybe for the first time. Anything's possible. I'm only eighteen, rather than: I'm eighteen and should have it all sorted. And all people are deserving of love, even me. I think. I told the psychiatrist what I've always thought about that, and, yeah... Work is ongoing.

I forgive people. Michelle. And Ross. They're not too difficult. Simone's a bit harder. I mean, she's never said sorry, never expressed any regret for her behaviour. But knowing what I know about her now, softens my feelings a little. My conception was a demented plan. Hers was worse. And I suspect she knows all about it just like I do.

⁓ℓℓ⁓

The day of my father's release from hospital coincides with my first allowed weekend home, so we're going to head back there together.

"The great serendipity of life," says Justin, all happy and funny as usual. There's more in his eyes, though, a sadness, something hidden and not spoken. I have a feeling this 'wisdom thing' I'm on will be temporary; it may in fact only be the meds making me think I'm all wise.

"Right," says Amalphia, sounding all decisive as we're all about to leave my father's room. "Could we all just sit down for a moment because there's something I want to say, and I want to do it while we're in a hospital in case it gives Aleks a shock."

We shuffle back into the room. My father, Will and Amalphia sit on the bed. Justin and I take the two chairs. Bubbles, here to support me today, sits on the armrest of my chair.

Amalphia puts her hands on Aleks's chest, feeling his heart. I know that's what she's doing.

"What is it, angel?" he asks.

She leans her head slightly to the side while gazing into his eyes, takes his hand and places it on her tummy.

"Really?" he asks, all smiles and surprise. This I don't get, this I can't see.

"No way!" says Will with a laugh. "Careless Christmas?"

"Phi! Not again..." admonishes Justin. "Crispin's right; you lot really are like rabbits up here."

Bubbles laughs and squeezes my hand. I hadn't realised she'd been holding it. And we all go home.

41

ALL ALONE IN THE garden, I walk past daffodils that are bending in the breeze. I might pick some when I come back. For Bubbles. She's coming to lunch today. When I reach the bottom of the path, I look back and see Amalphia and Aleks, my parents, watching me from the sitting room steps. My father lifts a hand and they turn away, retreating back into the room, giving me my privacy, knowing where I'm going this morning.

I walk up the side of the field where the crop is coming through, all green and spiky. I see the tips of the stones over the brow of the hill and quicken my pace to reach the circle. The place gives me time to catch my breath, to be calm, to get ready for the sight that waits on the other side of the woods. I haven't seen it yet. Everyone else has. And it's time I faced it too.

Almost time. I lie down on the flat stone and close my eyes. I feel the warmth of the sun. I feel the pinch of anxiety, almost dread. But I don't need to reach for anything chemical. It will be okay. It is okay.

The path between the pines seems the same, exactly the same, with all its little stones and roots and mossy bits and bright parts where the light comes through and darker places where it doesn't.

Here goes. I step out onto the castle lawn. I think it's the shock of it, but I laugh out loud. Really loud. I'm looking at several huge piles of blocks and rubble. Bits of the old castle walls remain standing here and there, several feet thick, several feet high. I can make out the outlines of the great hall and the tower. The newer extension that comprised theatre and pool is completely gone, reduced to a plain old heap of stones.

I stand on the grass and stare. The building firm Amalphia's hired to make the place safe has been hard at work. I know they had to take down walls and stuff because everything was unstable and dangerous. Huh. Just like I was. Like castle, like owner.

It's like a giant's come along with a dustpan and brush and tidied up. I try to make sense of the piles of stone that the clean-up crew have made. Where was the door? Why are even the steps no longer there? Maybe they've fallen in; I've been told that big chunks of the building just caved in and went underground. The dungeon is to be filled in with concrete.

I sit down on an enormous rectangle of stone and let myself think about the facts that have been lurking in the back of my mind.

The facts:

1. I'm an idiot. I cancelled all the different castle insurances. To save money.

2. I could have killed someone or someones with the fire I started.

3. I became an addict. Scratch that. I've learned that there is no past tense on this, like ever. I am one. I'm either in recovery or I'm not. But I am. In recovery. I'll always have to go to meetings, though. Always have to be careful.

4. Once upon a time, there was a beautiful castle here.

5. But that last fact is not strictly true.

209

I abandon the facts. They're all unchangeable now anyway. The castle may have been beautiful, but it was also a bit of a shithole. In many ways, that's what it was. The worst things in the world happened inside it. Below it.

The manuscript thing I put in Faye's room is being examined by excited experts. Looks like it was maybe written by Isobell Manteith, the Mermaid herself, about all she went through when she lived here. I don't think she'd be unhappy that the castle is gone. I don't think Michelle would be either.

Amalphia isn't. Unhappy, that is. And when she said 'no more secrets,' she really meant it. She's finally told the local council about the underground chamber, and an excited-sounding archaeologist is coming out to inspect it later this week.

It's time to leave the pile of stones and go home. It's feels like there isn't really much to see here. It'll all get sorted out. History enthusiasts and tourists are going to enjoy it now, not dance students, not damaged little boys. Is that what I am? Well, duh. But is it all I am?

There's one good fact I forgot to list: I fixed the Deil's Pool. I did that. It's all sparkly and light as I walk towards it today. Fair lights up the woods. That's what Ross said about it recently. During the same conversation where he explained that he loved Michelle. Like, really loved her. And it does, light up the woods, that is. The sun shines and reflects light all over the place on the water making me imagine beautiful things. Like mermaids on rocks. But as I get closer, she doesn't disappear, the mermaid. She turns and smiles at me, all bright and bubbly, her golden hair backlit by the sun.

"Is it as bad as you thought?" Bubbles asks, standing up on the stone.

"Bit nothing-y really," I tell her, and she nods.

She holds out her hands, daring me to leap out to her.

And I do.

ele

"Now look, there's to be no refusing these," says Amalphia, handing the three credit cards to me, Lexi and Ross. "I've made you extra cardholders on an account of mine. You don't have to use them, but if there's an emergency or an opportunity or an experience... anything. Feel free. Please. Take them for my peace of mind."

"Aye, we winna refuse 'at," says Ross, pocketing his card at once.

"Ah, you," she says to him, putting her hands on his arms and smiling sweetly up into his face. "You are the oldest, the most worldly-wise of this little group of travellers. You are charged with looking after the other two, the younger two. It's why I've given you that card."

"Aye, nae bother."

"I'm going to make you a promise," she tells him, maintaining eye contact all the while. "If anything – anything – bad happens to either of my boys on this trip, I will have you castrated."

He laughs. We all laugh.

"You can pretend I'm joking if you want," she says. "But I know people, and I have money. It'll never be traced back to me, and you'll never be the same again."

"Everything okay?" asks my father, frowning as he comes into the room.

"I've just been issuing last minute threats," Amalphia explains and we all laugh again, Ross a little less heartily than the rest of us. "Not to your babies, Aleks; don't worry."

"Mum!" says Lexi, not liking being called a baby.

Me, I don't mind this. I mind some things. I mind that Bubbles isn't coming with us like I wanted her to. She's not even going to join us when the student tour is over. I mind that she's fine with me travelling for maybe even a year. I more than mind. I thought her and me, well, you know. With my newly developed 'I deserve to be loved' idea, I thought things might be perfect all at once. But, I guess that was a bit stupid.

It's been sweet between us, though. We've been holding hands. Kissing. And somehow it feels more intimate than anything I've ever done before. Ever felt. It's like all those stupid clichés about someone being your other half or soulmate have actually become true for me. I feel like that with her. But maybe she doesn't. Or maybe she does.

When we spoke about me travelling, and us being apart for so long, she said: "If it's real, it won't change." Huh. "You need the space just now. Let's go our own way for a bit and see if we circle back to each other one day." And it's only now that I fully realise that this was her breaking up with me. Maybe not forever. And maybe it can be made right again. But for now: it's over. For now, we're properly apart. And that really, properly sucks.

"What's up?" Ross asks me now, puzzled. "Too late to back out, cousin. Taxi's here."

"You can call her from New Zealand," says Lexi, sensing what's up. "Send her a picture of a penguin."

"Buy her a cuddly toy one," adds Ross. "Girls like that."

"Yeah," says Lexi, all enthused with the idea. "Get her one that's holding a shiny red heart!"

"Okay, okay," I say, shoving my backpack into the boot of the taxi.

Quicker I do this, quicker I can come back to her and make things right, right?

42

One Year Later

The door's open. Just a little. Just enough for me to smell cake. And hear lots of people chatting. But it's not just me returning this time. Lexi and Ross feel no need to linger or delay or anticipate, but then the woman they love and haven't seen for over a year is not standing beyond this door.

So, in we burst. To applause. This family. Theatrical to the end. I'm smiling as I think it, though. I wouldn't have them any other way. I love all the hugs. Amalphia. My dad. Will. Faye. Anna. Sophia. David. Even wee Thomas, Amalphia's new baby, who I've never met before, smiles and seems happy to see me.

Then there's my friends. Ariel. Jonasz. Henry. Holly. More hugs and smiles.

I hug Justin and ask him how he is.

"Okay," he says, nodding, looking older. Greyer. Kian's cancer came back while we were away, and then, almost at once, it felt like, Kian was gone. He's just not here anymore. And I can't imagine what that's like for Justin.

It puts my worries in perspective. I mean, it's freaking me out a bit that Bubbles is not here. And that no one is mentioning or explaining her absence. But she isn't gone, gone. She's out there on this earth somewhere. In fact, she's up here in this area of Scotland. I know it. I mentally scan recent texts from her.

She's on summer break from the company and staying at Ariel's house. As is Henry. And he's here tonight, so why isn't she?

Alex with an x walks towards me on his little toddler legs and holds his arms up. "Zander x," he says as I lift him up. I've been gone for a year, and he still knows who I am. Clever kid that he is.

"We have a photo of all of us on the mantelpiece at home," explains Ariel. "He loves it."

Still. It's pretty impressive. He sits on my knee through some of dinner. He's had three operations while I've been gone. But he's strong and well. His sisters are totally hyper. They tear through the house playing with, or throwing around, every toy they can find. Amalphia jokes about the 'terrible twos' and tells us how energetic Alexei was at that age. I wonder what I was like. No one knows that. No one that's here tonight anyway.

After the pudding stage of dinner, the little girls conk out. Ariel puts them down in Amalphia's bedroom. Alex with an x is busy writing with crayons, so he stays with us.

"So," says Will, as we settle into a quieter, more reflective mode. But then he grins. Widely. At me. "You home for a rest, Alexander?"

Everyone laughs.

I just look at him: huh?

"You didn't copy Alexander in on those emails, did you?" says Ariel to Lexi, and, same as ever when she speaks to him, he goes bright red. Turns out he has good reason this time. She goes on: "Seriously, you should turn those things into a book. We were gripped! The drama! The excitement! The romance!"

She looks at me when she says this last bit, and again, my face says: huh?

"Don't tease him," says Amalphia. "We were all young once. Hot chocolate anyone?" And she gets up to make it.

"That's just what I said!" says Justin to Lexi. "The book idea. First thing that got me to smile, those emails. Only things that have made me laugh yet, truth be told. And I've got a few connections in publishing. We need to sit down and have a proper talk."

I'm about to ask the obvious 'WTF' question, but they all start off with their favourite bits. Of my brother's round-robin travel updates. That I knew nothing about.

"When you were island hopping in Thailand..." says Ariel, dissolving into laughter.

Jonasz picks up the tale. "Alexander hooked up with two girls on two separate islands?"

Ross joins in. "Oh aye, they ended staying on either side of us in beach huts. You were in hot water that day, cousin."

I want to say: not really my cousin. But I settle for just glaring at him.

"I liked the sound of the penguin lady best," says David.

"The penguin lady?" I ask, because, what the actual—?

"New Zealand," says Ross, nodding. "That quine could make the sound of every penguin species on the planet. And she did."

There's roars of laughter all round at that. I remember it rather differently. It was near the beginning. I was feeling lost. Down. Sore. She was there. She was kind and she was nice. And pretty. Yeah, that too.

"Enough." Thank you, Dad. I'm actually grateful for his strict teacher's voice, the one that people can't disobey. He continues: "Amalphia, you should tell them all about the castle."

I know most of what she tells us already, but it's a relief to be onto another subject. The castle ruins are all tidy and 'majestic looking' apparently. There's a posh new visitor centre, and it's busy with people every day.

"All my special things are there," says Faye. "So everyone can see."

I do not like that my little sister heard the earlier conversation. Or that so much was made of things that were not important. But I like hearing about the display of the harp, and the statue that we found in the pool, and even the old bed of the Mermaid and the Bear. But that makes me think of the person who is missing. My mermaid. Her absence hurts. Because, why isn't she here? She knew I was coming home tonight. She said it would be good to see me. I thought she was understating her feelings. Maybe she wasn't.

It's as my friends are leaving that this question is answered, this hurt deepened. I walk outside to wave them off, to help strap the sleepy toddlers into their car seats.

Henry hangs back a moment. Henry, who talks less than anyone I know, says more than anyone else did tonight. He tells me the truth: "She's seeing someone else."

43

THERE'S A PULSING, BLOODY, damaged mass of pain in my chest. I can't sleep. I don't want to eat. I want a painkiller, a really good one. But I won't do that again. People think I'm jetlagged. It's so bad, the chest thing, that I wonder if I've actually developed a heart condition. I mean, my dad had an underlying problem that he never knew about, so maybe I do too? But I know that's not it. I know that really. Though, a medical condition might be an easier fix.

Ariel is having a summer show with her ballet school in the village hall today. And I'm going. We're all going. I assume we're all going.

Yeah, all going: cars, village hall, then crowds and crowds of people. There's lots of excited and nervous parents and kids who are legitimately here for the show, and other opportunistic people just hoping to see Amalphia. Which they do, of course.

I'm excited to see someone too. Maybe I won't see her, though. Maybe she won't be here, and even if she is, maybe she won't want to see me. Maybe she's off out with the 'someone else.' No. I see her. And everything lights up around me and in me. Bubbles always does that. To a room or a building or even a stone circle. She's like a bright sun suddenly appearing in the dead of night.

She sees me. And she smiles. And then her smile wavers and her hand goes to her chest. As if she's in pain like me. But it can't be that. She quickly smiles widely again as we walk towards each other through the crowd.

"No one warned me you were tanned," she says. "You're completely devastating tanned. But you know that, right?" She leans her head to one side, the smile turning cheeky. "Yeah. You know it."

Fuck this crap. "You didn't tell me." I didn't actually mean to shout. Didn't mean to be angry at all actually.

"What?" she says, no longer smiling.

It's hard to say it, so I just repeat the information how Henry said it, the words coming out like sharp little bullets. "That you're seeing someone else."

Something happens. She seems to grow taller or harder or thinner or something. I don't know. And when she speaks, she doesn't sound like herself. "That's not the sort of thing we tell each other anymore, is it, Alexander?"

"Serena! Babes! It's about to start!"

We both look in the direction of the interruption, though I don't see the person that spoke. Bubbles smiles and does jazz hands, fucking jazz hands that I thought she didn't do anymore, and she walks off. She just walks off and leaves me standing there. Like an idiot.

She sits down on a chair in the front row. Beside some guy.

I sit on the chair nearest to me. And stare at them, Bubbles and the guy. It's like looking at the story of *Beauty and the Beast*. For real. He's got, like, really stupid hair, all sticking up everywhere; he must have to stand for hours in front a mirror doing it. He's fat-faced. And stupid looking. And speaking to her. And pressing his forehead against hers. And touching her face. And I want to punch him.

But I better not punch him. So I look at her. Just her. She's beautiful. She was always beautiful. But she's different now. She actually is taller or thinner or something. She's spent a year at the company. In the corps. It's been really tough. She told me that in her emails and texts: about the hours, and the competitiveness, and the joy of performing. Chatted on and on about that.

And look at her. Her hair's all up in some sort of shiny clasp. Simple. But sophisticated. She's like some sort of super model now. So she doesn't want me. I get that. The bloody pulsing mass and I, we're rolling with that. But, this guy? Her choosing him, I don't get. Aiden would've been better. At least he's striking or something. Isn't he? I don't know. Though maybe he wouldn't have been better.

The lights dim for the show to begin. But I can still see Bubbles. She's silhouetted against the little kids in coloured tutus. Her hair clasp catches the light now and then. I see her smile at him. I see him lean down and kiss her shoulder.

And then the show is over. And people are moving the chairs aside for the party afterwards. Well, I'm not staying for it. I'll find Ariel and tell her the show was great, which I'm sure it was, and—

"It's my fault, isn't it?" Lexi. He's suddenly at my side, pulling me to the edge of the room. "I fucked it up for you with Bubbles. Didn't I? With the emails?"

I look at him as people mill about all round us, carrying food and drink, whatever. I don't get it. And then I do. She got those emails. She read those emails.

My eyes blur. I shake my head.

He shakes his head too. "I was just trying to record it all and keep contact with home. You two were partying it up; I wrote it down. I didn't think."

Alexei is a quiet boy. Too quiet sometimes. He's really thoughtful and clever. Kian's death hit him hard. He cried for days when we heard about it. Ross and I made the decision not to leave him on his own after that. And this is not his fault.

"I thought you were telling her all about it too," he tells me now. "You texted her a lot, said you were telling her everything."

What a pair of shaking heads we are tonight. Because, no, I wasn't telling her everything. I sent her a fluffy toy penguin from New Zealand. How did that feel to her, arriving along with the travel update? Did they arrive together? Or did she get the penguin first and think, 'how cute?' And then she learned about me hooking up with a penguin expert. But it was meant to be cute, the toy. And none of the rest of it really meant anything. Really? Am I going to go to her with that cliché?

"Not your fault," I tell Alexei. "I did what I did. Didn't seem a big deal at the time. But it was. I hurt her."

Lexi wanders back to join the rest of the family, and I see the hair-gel guy offering Bubbles a plate of little cakes. She takes one. He looks at her adoringly. And I get it. She deserves to be adored.

I think about all the other gifts I sent her. Bunny. Teddy. Kangaroo. Parrot. She never said much about them. In fact, I remember thinking her work must have taken over her life, because that's all she wrote about. That, and to tell me my dad was doing well, and that she'd seen Justin. She went to Kian's funeral. Because she's a good person. More than that. She's perfect. She's beautiful. She's a goddess. Why did I ever leave? Why did I hook up with anyone else? Oh yeah, because I am a fucked-up mess. And an idiot. Always so scared of being alone. Always so stupid.

"What did that cake ever do to you?"

Get this. Hair-do guy is right here, in my face and talking to me. Bubbles is not with him, not at this moment. She must be in the bathroom or something. Or maybe she's left him. Yeah, right. Okay. I can do this.

"Alexander," I say, holding my non-cake-holding hand out to him. When did I take a cake? And why is this guy somehow familiar?

"Davin," he says, shaking my hand. Weak grip. And what sort of name is Davin? Not quite David, not quite Gavin. Make up your mind, dude. "I've heard a lot about you," he tells me.

Oh yeah? Like what? But I don't ask. I just say: "I've not heard anything about you." Though, all at once I realise that this is not true. I've heard his stupid name before, and I've seen him on the blog of the school tour. He was the new student. He was there with Bubbles when I wasn't. When I threw everyone out of the castle. And then he was there on the tour too.

"We only got together recently," he tells me now, going all gooey and pathetic looking. "She's great, isn't she? A real princess."

"That better not be me you're speaking about, Dav."

Bubbles is here. Right beside me. Right beside him.

"Because," she says. "I'm no princess."

"How about a warrior-style one?" he suggests, beaming at her with his fat round face.

"I'll consider it," she says with a smile.

He puts his arm round her.

And I can't.

Cant. Do. This. So, I don't.

I scrape the squashed cake off my hand and into the bin as I leave.

44

As soon as I'm outside the hall, I start walking. Walking. Walking. Walking. I walk right through the village, right on past the houses and shop and pub. On I go, ploughing right through the mud on the main road. It squelches under my feet. My shoes are ruined, but who cares? No one, that's who.

And then I've reached the place I somehow knew I was heading for. I'm standing in front of the castle gates and the statues of the Mermaid and the Bear. I walk through the gates and up the drive, towards the castle.

I know the castle's not gonna be there, but somehow I still expect to see it. And I do. It actually is still there. In a new way. Except it looks really old now. Ruined. I'm good at doing that to things. My speciality, that.

I walk right up to the ruin and step up onto a low bit of remaining wall and walk round on it. It's so strange that there's grass growing neatly where there used to be rooms. We danced between these walls once, all of us. Or actually, we danced up there in the sky. That's where the studios were. And down there, deep underground; all solid concrete now, of course.

I come to what I know is the great hall. The twelve long windows are still here in a remaining bit of thick wall. There's no glass left, of course; they're just elongated, pointy holes now. They still cast long shapes of light on the ground, though. The top of the wall is jagged and strangely shaped, a skeletal remnant of what was here before. A small metal sign tells me that this is where the fire originated, the one that destroyed the building. I bow to the sign with a hand flourish.

I'm lucky I wasn't charged and jailed and stuff. That guy, the one who interrupted Justin's wedding, he sorted it out. I had to give the castle and grounds away to the care of a trust, a different one this time, like giving the place back to the people. It showed I felt remorse and meant I got away with arson of my own house or something like that. I don't remember exactly. Diminished responsibility. A total nutter. A complete melt. Words from the time. Some other people's. Some mine.

I walk on.

Another metal sign tells me that I'm standing in the chapel. Huh. I look round. Try to get my bearings. This was more like the theatre, surely? When was there ever a chapel?

"Alexander."

An official-looking woman approaches. I guess she's come out of the modern visitor centre over beside the trees. How did she know who I was? Am I famous? Is there a 'wanted' sign with my face on it up in the square-looking visitor centre? Is the woman here to chase me off the property?

The light catches her name badge and I read it:

Simone Manteith ~ Castle Manager

No way.

She stands there looking at me.

I stand here looking at her.

She says: "I am so sorry."

I don't say anything. Where is this going?

"For everything," she says, with actual tears running down her face. "The castle burnt down, and I thought you might be dead. I could see it, you see, the light of the fire. From my cottage. The smoke spread for miles. I could smell it, and I walked towards it. I walked and walked. And then I saw it, all burning and smoking and terrible, but you were all gone by then. And I didn't know you if were alive for a long time. It felt like a long time."

I continue to just look at her. I'm not sure what to do with any of this.

"The castle burnt down, and I grew up," she goes on. "That's how it feels. To me. But you. You, Alexander. You got the worst of me. And I can't take it back. I can't take any of it back. All I can do is tell you that I am so very sorry. And I wish I could take it all back and do it over and be different, be better."

And I know she does. She is actually sorry. But, she's also right. It doesn't take it back. But it does do something. Somewhere deep in the bloody mass, something shifts a bit.

"You could have me charged with child abuse," she continues. "I would plead guilty and admit it all. Or I could just hand myself in and tell the police everything. I'll do whatever you want me to do. I thought about just going ahead and doing it, but I didn't know if you would want it all out there in public record. This is about what's best for you now."

I experience a small flare of victory, a moment of long longed-for vengeance come true. Everybody would know the whole truth, the radiator, everything. Simone would be judged and hated and shamed. The feeling passes as I look at her, the other damaged child of the Manteith family. It's like our old roles have reversed, and I have the power over her now. And I'm surprised to find that I don't want it; I really don't. What would reporting her involve? It would be a stressful nightmare, and I think we've all had enough of those. At least for now. It feels like something to take time over and discuss with my family, but not right this minute, not today. Not for a while actually.

"I'll have to think about it," I say.

She nods. "Of course. You can let me know anytime, or you can just make a complaint to the police. I will respect whatever you do."

"There's one thing you can tell me, though," I say and she looks at me in anticipation. "What did 'Like, mother, like son,' mean? You said it about the radiator."

Simone is always pale, but she goes even paler now. She shakes her head. "I'm sorry, Alexander. More sorry than I can say. But I don't know. I don't remember saying that. I drank a lot back then, and it's all a bit of a blur."

"Oh."

"I was probably trying to lord it over you about me knowing who your real mother was."

"Oh," I say again.

A weird silence develops as we both stand there looking at what's left of the castle.

"Will you let me show you something?" she says after a while, sounding hesitant, fearful even, still looking super pale.

I nod again, still silent, like I'm in some sort of strange trance, and I follow her round the back of the castle ruins. There used to be a garden here. I'm not sure why there isn't now. Did it go up in flames too?

Simone leads me to a shiny new gravestone. She tells me it's the grave of an unnamed woman. Simone babbles on, sounding a bit more like her old mad self, but not quite. She says the grave was discovered by archaeology students last summer, and that it's thought it might be linked with the witch trials in the 16th century, and it may even be the resting place of a young woman mentioned by Isobell Manteith in her writings, the writings that I saved.

I smile. "And by saved, you mean I didn't incinerate them along with everything else?"

"Yes," says Simone, quite seriously, adjusting some of the flowers on the grave. "Amalphia comes here," she tells me, as if proud of the fact. "She left these flowers the other day."

The visitor centre, where we go next, feels completely surreal. It's grey and boring on the outside and all shiny with glass panels everywhere inside. There's a strange, new plastic-y smell to the place. All the stuff I found in the pool is on display. The broken bits of glass are pieced together into an angel window; the statue of the Virgin Mary has pride of place in the centre of the room. Apparently she's called 'Our Lady of Aberdeen.'

Then there's the harp from the house. And the old bed. I touch the carving of the mermaid.

"I've really fucked things up with Bubbles," I find myself telling Simone. And we talk about it. Over tea and chocolate digestive biscuits, between mermaids and bears and golden crucifixes, we just talk. Which, when I think about it, is all very weird. Only it isn't. It doesn't feel weird.

By the time I'm walking past the pool to go back home, I've agreed, happily agreed, to come back tomorrow and join in a tour of the ruins to learn more about the history of the Manteiths. Where I came from. Where she came from. Where do the two of us go from here? Who knows? I guess I'll decide in time.

Where I'm going in my life is another mystery. There'll be no tour guide to show the way. But, for just now, I watch the sunlight on the pool and the dragonflies as they fly up and down, again and again, in their happy dance of summer.

45

I SLEEP REALLY WELL. I wake feeling different. I don't know how exactly, still sad, still not knowing what to do, but in some undefined sort of way: better. I decide there'll be no thinking of the present or the future today. I'm going back to the past with Simone and her visitor tour. It'll be like a holiday. A really fucked-up holiday. Because, you know, I haven't had enough of a break. I'm smiling to myself at that thought as I run down the stairs and crash – splat! – into Davin.

Davin. 'Dav,' as Bubbles called him yesterday. 'Hair gel on a stick' is here in my home? And then I see Bubbles behind him. Ariel too, and Henry. They're here to do class, they tell me. Fucking class with Will. And my dad. And Amalphia.

My parents were talking about that last night, about wanting to get fit, stay fit, how they were going to do class every day in the upstairs studio here in the house from now on. I was staring out into the garden at the time and didn't really listen. I was still thinking about Simone. And the castle. The things I'm supposed to be thinking about today.

"Why don't you join us?" says Ariel as we all stand in the small space of the stairway, my position meaning I'm basically blocking their way.

Their faces seem eager as they look back at me, awaiting my answer. But are they? Does Bubbles really want me, the guy who hurt her, invading her space during class? Also: I've not done class for ever. And Davin is a professional dancer. Or is he? I don't know if he's gone on to work in dance. I saw him on the blog but I don't remember if he was any good. He obviously wasn't memorable. I can't see any dancer grace about him. But he might still show me up.

"Be like old times," says Henry.

But I don't think it would. "I'm meeting Simone," I tell them.

"By choice?" asks Bubbles, looking properly concerned.

"Yeah," I tell her. "It's different." And I want to tell her it all, about how Simone suggested I could have her charged, about the unnamed woman's grave, and about the castle, because I think she would get it. She would be interested. She is already. But this is not the time. And maybe it never will be.

So I look away from her, turn side on and squeeze past everyone on the stairs. Will's in the hall, scrolling through a playlist on his phone.

"Are you teaching them today?" I ask him.

He nods. "Should I go easy on 'em?"

"Nope," I say at once. Show Davin up, why don't you? That's how much of a dick I am. The guy's done nothing wrong. I've done everything wrong. And I really need to stop now.

Will salutes me and runs up the stairs. And I run out of the house.

ele

They found a medieval chapel under the castle theatre. It's where my angel window and probably the statue of the Madonna, as Simone calls her today, came from. Some of the old chapel floor is left. Big flagstones sit bared in the middle of the grass.

And underneath the swimming pool? They found a Celtic roundhouse. A really big one. That's like going back thousands of years. They've found weapons and jewellery and a carved stone-ball thing. The balls are often found near stone circles and may be linked to them in some way. It's mysterious and exciting. Simone is good at explaining it all to the tour group and getting us all enthused too. Is she trying extra hard to show she's a valued member of the community? Someone who shouldn't be reported to the police? I don't know. I'm not sure she's clever enough to do that.

After the other visitors have wandered off to walk round the ruins by themselves, Simone shows that perhaps she is more intelligent than she seems. She tells me she's doing a degree in history and says that I could do something like that too if I wanted. I'm clever. So she says. But I don't know. About any of it.

I wonder if class is finished at the house. I wonder if they've all gone home, Bubbles and Davin especially. I kinda don't want to go back into the middle of them. And I can feel the pull of the stone circle. Or maybe I'm just imagining that as an excuse to delay going home. Whatever, I set off up the unchanged path. And then I run. As fast as I can. I jump a tree root. I race into the circle glade. And there's Bubbles standing on the flat stone, hair all golden and messed in the breeze, no longer tied back, face all shining and full of something, some emotion, something strong, something fierce even.

I want to run at her, grab her, and kiss her. Like, I want to so much it's taking all my strength not to do it. Because I don't have that right. It would be a violation. I know I've messed up in other ways, but I'll never hurt her like that.

"I thought you might walk home this way," she says. "And I thought we could talk."

"Cool," I say, backing away further from her, like I'm scared to hear what's coming. I lean against the big recumbent stone and brace myself.

"Right," she says, uncertain too maybe, sitting down on her stone.

"I never meant to hurt you," I say. So, cliché number one is out of the way then. "It didn't mean anything, any of it." Number two: check. "I was just looking to feel," – what exactly, you monumental melt? – "better." Ugh. Now I sound sleazy.

"You don't have to explain anything to me, Alexander. I realise you didn't know Alexei was sending me those emails. And we weren't actually a couple, were we?"

"We were something."

She nods, real fast, and says: "Something I can't cope with."

What's that supposed to mean? Nothing good, obviously. I actually want to cry. To sit on the ground and bawl like a small child.

"Don't be sad," she says. "Oh, that's a stupid thing to say; we all feel what we feel. But I don't want you to be sad."

"I don't want that either," I say, squeezing the words past the swelling in my throat. "For you."

"I know," she says. "And I have to be careful not to be too sad or too happy. I will always have to watch that. Like you'll always have to watch substances. It's like..." She turns away a bit and holds her face up to the sun. "If I were to hear about Davin being with someone else like that, it would be like getting a blister from pointework. Sore. Stingy. Might bleed a bit. But with you..." She lowers her head and her hands form small fists in her lap. "With you it's like being injured so badly that I could never dance again. Bones, tendons, muscles, all shredded. Organs burst. Heart shot out."

Fuck.

She stands. She looks right at me. She stares at my face. "I know it sounds mad with all I've just said, but looking at your face still makes me feel calm. It always has." She holds out her hand. "Friends?"

I walk forward and take her hand, but I don't shake it. I'm agreeing that we're friends, yes, but I'm not sealing some deal to only ever be that. If there's a chance she could be the right amount of happy with me, I'm not giving up on that. Not yet.

She says she has to go. She takes her hand back. And I know she needs to be by herself for a bit now.

So I don't follow her. But this is not over. I have a feeling it's only just begun.

46

"Is he any good?" I ask my dad as we're laying the table for dinner. I'm about to explain who I mean, but it turns out I don't need to.

"No," he says at once. "I made a mistake when I accepted him into the school. His stance, his arms; both these revealed that he had not had the benefit of properly trained teachers. I thought he had a deep determination about him, but I was wrong." He pauses. "You are superior in every way." He smiles and raises an eyebrow at me.

So, next morning, I'm doing class. For the first time in like forever. And it's good. Really good. I'd forgotten that I actually like the way it feels, to move my body to the music, to stretch out in the longest line possible, to be my best self. My best dancing self, anyway.

I tried a few exercises last night in my room, you know, just to make sure I hadn't seized up on the other side of the world. And I hadn't. I'm almost thankful to Simone and the mad stretching routine that she imposed when I was a kid – almost, not actually – because I'm still supple. I don't think I'll ever lose it.

Music echoes across the upper level of the house. This studio is not so dusty, though. It's warm. It's home. Papa Zolotov is teaching today, and he was completely right about Davin. It's not dislike or jealousy clouding my judgement. Ballet, I know, and the guy has no line, no grace, no flexibility. Some strength maybe. But by itself, that's just, what? Unimpressive, that's what.

The studio is sunny. The windows provide an amazing view of the countryside. I can see the grey stones of the stone circle in the distance as I plié at the front of the barre.

When we turn to the other side, I see everyone else. Ariel: a little out of shape but still got it. Henry: better than I've ever seen him. Will: wild and contemporary in style even in this classical class. Amalphia is like me in that she hasn't lost the bendiness, and she's kinda regal looking in a long black ballet skirt. Davin, I barely look at. Except that Bubbles is beside him.

Bubbles is perfect. Stunning. Legs as high as mine. They didn't used to be. She really did throw herself into work. I wasn't wrong about that. Was it because I hurt her? Or am I being a self-centred jerk for thinking that? I know she always wanted this, to be really good. And I'm glad for her. The glad feeling burns inside the pulsing pain of my heart. But there's light and warmth here too. Because, in this moment, I'm close to her. We're in the same room, doing the same thing, and it's good. And this class seems to be playing to all my strengths.

There are no mirrors up here, but I can see my legs go up; I can feel the fine curve of my arms in port de bras and the height/strength thing I got going once Amalphia took over my training when I was, what, eight? It's still there, baby. Yeah, it is! My father high fives me after a grand allegro that combined all the jumps I've always been best at.

Amalphia bows out of class early. Says she's exhausted. But she's back at the end with hot drinks and cake. That's the kind of dancers we are in this family. And Davin's not okay with it. Really not okay with it. He looks at the cake like it's poison. And I actually feel a bit of empathy for the guy. He must know he's not that great a dancer, so he definitely can't risk gaining any weight. Me? I eat what I want. I burn it off. So that must suck for him. Mind you, he has Bubbles. He sits right up close to her on the floor after class and rubs her shoulders. So, there's that.

A party atmosphere develops. We all sit round on exercise mats, eating and drinking and talking about our feet and our legs. I compliment Bubbles on her improved extension.

"Thanks," she says without any vanity. Well, duh; that's not in her. "So, are you getting back into it?" she asks. "Ballet? Dance?"

No, I'm mainly here to see what's going on with you and your new boyfriend. To see if he's the one who can make you happy. If he is, I'll bow out. But I don't say any of this out loud. Obviously. I shrug. "It's what I'm doing today."

"You know Crispin wants you for a film," says Justin who arrived up here with Amalphia and the cake. "So do I, for that matter. We're thinking of doing another historical. A full-length feature this time. Big Hollywood thing. We're after you too, darling," he sides at Bubbles. "But these cheekbones." He takes my chin in his hand. I feel a bit like the skull in Hamlet. "They could cut ice, or cake, or cheese; what is the expression? Melt hearts, anyway... You'd be wasted in the ballet studio and just being seen from the stage. The big screen could do big things for you."

It's another little spark in the dark mess of my splatted heart. Bubbles and I could work together again? Maybe? Even just discussing it feels good.

"Bubbles was amazing as the Mermaid," I say because it's true, and I don't like that she was dismissed and forgotten in Justin's cheekbone speech.

"I fell in love with her before I ever met her, seeing how beautiful she was in that," says the human hair dryer called Davin. He's blowing hot air there because he's not acknowledging the awesome person she is, or her talent, only her looks.

"We visited dark places together during the filming," I say, looking at her, remembering the dungeon, remembering Justin's reaction to the place, understanding all sorts of things now and wishing I hadn't started this conversation.

"I haven't forgotten," says Bubbles, looking straight back at me, and I think she means something else. Like maybe her grandfather's funeral? And, again, I wish I hadn't reminded either of us of any of it. She smiles. "How is Simone?"

I grin back. Oh. She's referring to the time we trashed Simone's house. "She seems a lot more together these days," I say.

"She does, doesn't she?" says Amalphia. "I meant to warn you she might be there, before you visited the place. I hope it wasn't a terrible shock?"

I shake my head. "She's apologised to me," I say, without thinking where I'm going again. "For it all. And given me some stuff to think about. It's weird. But it kinda feels a bit better."

"Good," say Amalphia and Bubbles together, and the others all agree: good, good, good.

But I feel like I want to cry, and this is not the place. I'm supposed to be being impressive. Amalphia distracts everyone with cake, and Will says he wants me to look at something on the computer in his room which is just off the studio. So: saved.

"You all right?" he asks as we stand in front of the computer but don't actually look at anything on it.

"Yeah, it's just a bit weird," I tell him. "Not the look I'm going for today."

"I wouldn't worry about that," he says, leaning his head toward the studio where Bubbles is looking this way, full of concern and completely ignoring the chattering guy at her side.

Crap. I didn't mean to actually manipulate her. Especially not with anything that really matters, like deep stuff. Seeing her like this, among a group of ballet people, reminds me of the first time I ever saw her, met her. It was our first day as students at the castle. I'd been worried that everyone might be snobby or judge me for being the headmaster's son. She smiled at me, so open and friendly, and then when she danced across the studio in class, she was so bubbly. I gave her the nickname. And she liked it. And I realise, it's always been her. Chantal may have matched me better in trouble-making ways back then, and then Ariel with her murderous-mother past, but it was actually always Bubbles who had my heart. I was just too deep in my own mess to see it for a while.

But they're all going now anyway. So I try to cheer up and look happy to say goodbye.

"You went full out, didn't you?" notes Ariel as I arrive back in the studio. "In class?"

"Yeah," I say. Why wouldn't I? I was out to impress.

"You're gonna pay for it tomorrow," she says.

"Nah, I'm always fine next day."

"We'll see," she says, and off down the stairs they go.

47

I HEAD TO THE pub with Aleks and Will in the evening. Dad and Dad as I suppose they are. We're talking about their upcoming vow renewal. It's going to take place in the stone circle, and be like an old-fashioned handfasting. One of the old castle people, Sun, is coming to do it. I remember her from both real life and the earlier files on Michelle's laptop. I look away from the dads, unsettled by the memory, and find myself staring directly into the eyes of Gail from the Christmas party a year and a half ago. Gail, the girl who I deliberately used to get the hotel key, and then walked out on and never bothered to seek out and apologise.

"I'll just be a minute," I say and walk over to the bar.

Gail glowers as I approach.

"I'm really sorry for how I treated you," I tell her. "I was completely messed up at the time. What I did to you was completely messed up too. And I'm sorry if it hurt you."

She agrees it was messed up. But she smiles anyway. Says she knows I've done worse since, and I end up with a pint on the house.

"And we thought it was all about Bubbles," says Will as I sit back down at the table.

"It is," I say with no hesitation, accidently revealing my heart. "I was just saying sorry for something from before."

"So, Serena, she got the emails," says my father. "And she thinks—"

"Thinks?" says Will with a grin. "Doesn't the situation remind you of me and Malph back in the day?"

"What do you mean?" I ask.

"I had a lot of casual hook ups when I was younger," he explains. "Before we were ever a thing. And I didn't think she knew anything about it. And she didn't. Until Bevan told her, that is." The two men share an empathetic look. "She once accused me of sleeping with every woman in the castle except her."

"Well, you almost did," says my father, laughing.

Will frowns. "Nah, Holly and me have always stayed platonic."

"Who else did you sleep with?" I ask, intrigued. I mean, I've seen them all now, everyone who was at the castle in the past.

"Sadie," Will says.

I find this hard to believe. "Sadie of 'Gavin and Sadie?'"

He nods. "Malph caught me coming out of her room near the beginning of us being up here, just when I'd wondered if we might get together. I was such a walking hormone. It was such a bad moment."

"It worked out well for me," my father says, raising a glass.

"It's not the same," I say. "With Bubbles. She thinks I can hurt her too much. Make her too sad or too happy. You know, with her mental health. She told me that."

"And what do you think?" It's my father that voices the question, but they both look at me like the answer is really important which, I suppose, it is.

I tell the truth. "I think I get her, and I know how to be around her when she's feeling out of whack. I think I would see ups and downs coming. I hope I would anyway. I would always support her in whatever way she needed. And I would never hurt her. Not again."

"Because?" That's Will.

Heartbeat. "I love her." And now I've gone red. My face is hot. My hair is hot. My neck, my knees, my ears. Ugh. But they don't tease me about it.

"There is only one thing that ever really works," my father says. "You have to tell her how you feel and be honest about all the rest too. With us, Amalphia and I, when I did this, it was a relief for us both. I told her of my great shame, how I had wanted this life, to be married, to have children, when she was so young and at the start of her career. And she was relieved because she had thought something much worse was going on."

"What?" I ask. "What did she think was going on?"

"Well..." My father is hesitant. Is there really more I don't know?

Will is direct as ever. "She thought he'd been shagging Michelle again."

"Oh." Oh. I think I know when this was.

But I don't want to think about it, about any of that back then. So I think about Bubbles instead. I think about being completely honest and open with her. "Well, maybe after class tomorrow. Maybe I'll get to speak to her then."

48

BUT, THE NEXT MORNING, class doesn't happen. First I think it's not going to happen for me because when I wake up, I can barely move. My legs have stopped working. Completely! Well, not completely. I ease myself across the room and to the bathroom. I stand in a hot shower, willing my muscles to ease out and work properly again. But, realistically, I'm going to be so crap in class, I think I should just skip it. Or, maybe I could sit with ice packs and watch?

I'm still mulling this over when Davin arrives at the house. My parents are upstairs getting ready for class. I'm sitting eating toast in the kitchen by myself. And he's all by himself too. I perk up. Even my legs feel a bit better.

"What's up?" I ask him. "Where are the others?"

"Oh, Ariel got a letter," he tells me. "From her mum or someone. Big fuss." And then, the absolute tosser, he rolls his eyes. "But I can't miss class," he says. "I'll never get a job if I do that, so I guess it's just you and me today."

"Guess again," I say as I text Will to say I'm taking his car and going to Ariel's. He won't mind.

Davin heads on up the stairs, and I walk outside to the old 4X4. I put the car in gear, push through the pain of my creaky legs, and roll away down the drive to go support my friend.

ele

There's a police car parked outside Ariel's house. My heart is pounding, bloody mass put aside for just now, because: what's happening? To Ariel, to Bubbles, to little Alex with an x?

Jonasz meets me at the door, thanks me for coming, confirms there was a letter, a really nasty letter, but that nothing else has happened and that everyone is through in the kitchen. He really means everyone; it's a crowd. Apart from Bubbles and Henry, and Ariel and Jonasz and the babies, there's also two police officers – a man and a woman – and Jonasz's parents and brothers.

Ariel hugs me, little Alex in her arms.

He immediately reaches for me: "Zander x, Zander x," he says and snuggles into my neck when I take him.

I get it. He's upset. He can feel the worry of all the people around him but doesn't understand what it's about. I walk away from the crowd with him, over to the kitchen window, and we look out over the fields and sloping hills. I give little Alex my phone, let him play with the music on it. That pleased him at dinner the other night, and it does again now.

"Look at you two," says Bubbles, coming over and putting a hand on each of our backs.

"We're buddies," I tell her.

"I can see that. Horrible thing, this." She indicates the police with her eyes.

"What did the letter say?" I ask. "Isn't she still locked up somewhere?"

"Yes, she's in proper prison now, remember? The police checked, and she's still there. Letter was just bile. Telling Ariel her kids are, well. ." She lowers her voice to a whisper. "That they shouldn't have been born, that they'll be malformed freaks with nothing to offer, just like she is. That no one else in the family wants to have kids in case they turn out like these little guys. Can you believe that?"

"Of Ariel's mother? Yeah."

"And the thing is," says Bubbles, pausing as if it's too much to speak past the outrage she feels. "The kids are amazing! They're fantastic. It's like the woman needs to put down beauty or goodness or joy. She has to butt in and spoil it." Her eyes have teared up.

I put my free arm round her. "She can't spoil it. She can just cause upset, but it won't last. She'll be watched more carefully from now on, surely? She's unlikely to find a way to have fun like this again. So the laugh's really on her."

"Yes," she says. "But Ariel really needs us just now. I'm so glad you came, Alexander. Clinton's coming too. The dance initiative he works for have only just gone on break. He was going to be coming up in a few days anyway to stay and do class, but he's arriving later today after hearing about this."

"Good," I say. Clinton's always been close with Ariel, and it'll be good to see him.

"Will you stay too?" Bubbles asks me.

"Sure, if that's, you know, what everyone wants."

"It is," says Bubbles with no hesitation, and neither of us mention Davin or where he is.

Putting my jealous feelings about the guy aside and trying to be fair, could he have been removing himself from something he felt was a family matter? Maybe, but that's not the reason he gave me.

The police leave, taking the letter with them.

"Now, you're not to worry about this," says Janet, Ariel's mother-in-law. "Maxine's always got to have her claws into someone. And she's managed to sneak a letter out. That's all. Would you like us to stay?"

Ariel and Jonasz insist that, no, they do not need their family to stay, but they do want the rest of us there. Ariel feels safety in numbers, secure with all her friends around.

There's mashed potato lunches for the babies. Henry and I help feed them.

Bubbles goes for a walk with Davin as soon as he returns. So she's gone, away off out with him. I wonder if she's showing him Ariel's tower. I remember the two us being up there early one morning. Not the best of times either actually. But still. We were together. Close.

And now we're watching kids' TV. And it's surreal. Literally. Like it's set in some nightmare universe. But the babies love it. There's going to be a Chinese takeaway later once they're in bed. And films. And Clinton!

He walks in, and the atmosphere cheers up at once. "The Cavalry is here!" he announces, and we all cheer. Alex with an x claps.

"Better get you boys some beds sorted," Jonasz tells us. "You'll have to share."

As we make our way through the bedroom area of the house, Jonasz points out where everyone's sleeping.

"Bubbles is in there," he tells me. "Dandini's further down the hall."

"Dandini?" I ask.

"Well, he looks like a character out of a pantomime, doesn't he? Davin, I mean."

I laugh. Yeah, I suppose he does. But this is news. They're not sleeping together. This brings me an inordinate amount of happiness as I accept the bottom bunk below Clinton. Even his fart warnings don't dent the happy.

And by the time we get back downstairs, Jonasz and Davin are heading out. Jonasz is driving Davin to the bus stop. I don't ask Bubbles why this is. I don't pry. She's sitting by the fire with the little cat on her knee, stroking its fur rhythmically. I know she's upset. I know she's calming herself down. I've seen it before. With Aiden. Another useless prick.

"D'you want a cup of tea?" I ask her, and she looks up.

Her smile is so warm it burns right into me, easing the pain in my heart, and I know – I just know – that everything's gonna be okay.

49

THAT OKAY FEELING. IT'S so strong. The word okay doesn't even describe it. It's like, I can see that it's sunny outside but it doesn't matter, because it's so much better in here. No, that's not it. It's a rightness. A belonging. Clichés. They just seem to happen with Bubbles. And I am lying in bed with her. Not in a romantic way. Not really. And definitely not in a sex way.

She invited me in to her room here at Ariel's last night. To talk. And wow, did we? Half the night. I told her the thing I've not told her before: about my past feelings for Amalphia. Because Bubbles should know all of my dark. It'll never be right otherwise, knowing I've kept a secret from her.

"You were a messed-up kid, Alexander," she says, accepting it, accepting me, and I'm so relieved. I relax more than I think I've ever relaxed in my whole life.

She told me that she dumped Davin. Walking out when Ariel needed everyone was the end of him for her. She told me how her mum and little sister are living in Aberdeen now; they've got their own flat, away from her nasty dad. I'm so glad about that and about how happy Bubbles is about it too. She's going to stay with them after things calm down here at Ariel's.

We talk about that too. Ariel's mother. Bubbles is worried that the incident has caused a dip in Ariel's self-esteem. Ariel used to be made to feel like shit by her mother, and that's snuck in a bit again with the letter. We're going to try to make sure it's healed quick.

I tell her about travelling, what it was really like; you know, not a shag a minute.

"Alexei hero-worships you," she says. "At one point he wrote that you and Ross were living the dream while he was just writing it down."

That gets me. Because it's so not true. He's the well balanced one. I'm a bit of a nut-job.

"You know that's a really offensive term?" says Bubbles.

"Even if it's about myself?"

"Especially if it's about you," she says and lays her head on my chest.

And that's how we go to sleep. And here we still are in the morning.

"Sorry," I tell her when she wakes, all golden curls across her face. "We fell asleep."

"It's okay," she says. "We have done this before, remember."

Yeah, we have. At the castle, in Michelle's old room. Near the Laird's Lug and the secret stairway. Places that don't exist anymore. Which is a weird thought. But we still exist. We're still living and breathing, just as we were then. Though back then there was usually some crisis going on with one of the two of us. This is just calm and natural and not what everyone else obviously thinks it is at all.

Because they're all thinking it. They're all smiling. Over a breakfast of butteries (local salty roll things) and coffee, I know they're all assuming stuff. They're wrong, but at least everyone is happy today.

Ariel's sadness from yesterday has been replaced by a fierce and protective anger. For her babies. For herself. For all of us. "I'm going to have her charged," she says. "With whatever they can charge her with. She's not supposed to ever contact any of us, so there must be something we can do."

We all agree, yes, she should do that.

"And my kids are the best kids in the world!" We all applaud at that, even little Alex with an x. "Seriously, they are," she goes on. "They're more advanced than any of the other children at the toddler group. And I'm not just saying that because they're mine; they really are!"

Ariel's Grandmother arrives as we're clearing the table. We all sit back down to hear what she's got to say. Jonasz gets her a buttery and a strong cup of tea.

"I went to see Maxine yesterday afternoon," she tells us, looking quite scary. "She won't be doing anything like that again. She had the nerve to say how she longs to see the babies, how it's so unfair that she doesn't get to, as if she's the victim in all this. I fluctuated from feeling that she hadn't changed at all to thinking she's more delusional than ever. Extra security's in place, though; don't you worry." Her face changes completely as she puts her hand on Ariel's, and she's a nice grandmotherly lady again.

We all go out to lunch at the local carvery with 'Ganny Patti' as little Alex calls his great grandmother. Jonasz's family are there too.

We stay at Ariel's for three more days, all of us, then, after class on Monday, Ariel tells me it's okay if I want to stay at home now. The drama is over. Peace and serenity have returned to their lives. I'm going to miss the night-time talking and sleeping arrangements, because they continued for the three nights too.

"I might stay on a bit," says Bubbles. "I would like to see the castle and Simone. Though it might be a bit awkward given that the last time we met was at the wedding, and I gave her a right mouthful."

"That was before the fire," I say. "I told you she's a bit different now."

"I know, but I want see it for myself."

We wander along the path by the pool. We watch the dragonflies do their dance. Bubbles loves them. She tells me that.

"I love them too," I say, because I do.

Simone gives us biscuits and tea in the visitor centre.

"Do you think you'll ever have children?" Bubbles asks her, and I realise that this is important. I can't believe I didn't think of it before. Simone, regardless of what growing up she's done, should not be in charge of a child again.

"Oh no," Simone tells her, possibly understanding the point. "I've made sure of it; had my tubes tied last year. And I'll never let myself be in a situation where I'm looking after someone else's child either. Except here in educational groups with teachers and parents present. I promise you that."

Bubbles nods and says she's off to explore the castle.

"She's lovely, isn't she?" Simone whispers to me as the two of us watch Bubbles walk along the remains of a wall, arms held out at the side for balance.

"Yes," I say, because she is.

We visit the grave of the unknown woman, and Bubbles promises to come back with flowers. Another day.

Bubbles and I walk the uphill path through the pines and lie on the biggest stone of the stone circle. We kissed here two summers ago. We don't do that now. We talk. So much. We always seem to be connected somewhere, though: hands, heads, spooning. And that's okay. This is us now, and I love it. I love her. I love us.

I tell her about some of the stuff I saw on Michelle's old laptop in the castle. She wants to know. She wants to understand. I tell her about Michelle's father who was also Simone's father and grandfather.

"That's not what happened to me," she tells me. "Don't think that."

So I don't think it. But I'm glad. We're slow and gentle, and though every so often, especially when I'm alone, I get freaked out, because: what are we doing? I'm falling in deeper than ever, and though we talk all the time, we have not talked about this, about what we're doing, what we are, or what we feel about each other... I'm okay. It's okay. We're okay.

It's summer in Scotland with all its dragonflies and butterflies and picking ticks off each other at night. We do those clichés of watching the sun set and, more occasionally, the sun rise. We swim in the woodland pool and get covered in mud.

Bubbles leaves to stay with her mum and sister, but she's coming back next week for the handfasting, vow-renewal thing.

I give her Michelle's locket before she goes.

Amalphia found it in the dungeon that night, the night of the fire. She grabbed it and ran out of there and through the tunnel, through the chamber that Ross had left open for airing; she ran up into the house and through the woods and back to my father, and me

It's had a lot of adventures, this necklace. And now it should belong to the Mermaid of the castle again. And that's who Bubbles is. Whatever we go on to become or not become.

She fastens it round her neck. And she waves goodbye.

I go home. I walk upstairs. I stand at the barre on the top level of the house. I look out across the fields at the stones. And I smile.

50

WE ALL GATHER IN the garden: the bride, the grooms and the bride's people and best men. We could be from any time really, well not any time, medieval most likely. The boys are all wearing white lace-up Highlander shirts, and the girls are in white dresses, except Amalphia who's in bright red.

"Right," says Justin. "We're all going to make our way up there now, and Phi, Hearst and Zolotov are going to wait for a short moment only, and then follow. Everyone's waiting; let's not have them get bored before we've even begun."

"It's not a performance, Justin," says Amalphia, beaming at him.

His eyes narrow. "I recognise that expression, Treadwell, and I'm issuing a rule: no sex before marriage. Not today. If I look round and you're not following, I'm coming back to get you!"

"Time for a quickie then," says Will, earning himself a glare.

Justin swings round to lead the way, baby Thomas strapped to his chest, and off we go, down the garden and up the side of the field. The sun is hot on our faces, the earth hot on our bare feet. Justin checks that the parents are following and we march on and up, through the kissing gate, and into the stone circle.

Everyone cheers as we arrive. Bubbles comes over and touches the flower on my shirt. She's got one in her hair. It makes her seem more than human, like a fairy or goddess of the circle. She steps back as my parents arrive to massive applause.

Sun, their old castle friend, walks forward to meet them, and everything begins.

Bubbles re-joins me and takes my hand. And we're off, in a huge circle dance, round and round and round we go. It's dizzying. It's fun. We're all laughing and stumbling about, and I'm feeling: why don't we do things like this more often? Life would be better; life would be great, if we just danced like this a lot more.

We all sit down in a circle round the grooms and bride. The three of them gather small pink and white flowers from around the grass and put them in each other's hair. I find one near me and give it to Bubbles. She puts it in my hair.

I pull my gaze away from Bubbles. Sun is speaking. About handfasting. The history of it. And how it lasts for a year and a day, the commitment. She goes on about Amalphia, Aleks and Will and their trailblazing relationship. We all applaud that.

And then: the vows. Amalphia, my mother, my really real mother, steps up onto the flat stone and goes first.

"Aleks. Will." She pinches the area between her eyes and nose. I think she's trying not to cry. "This could be short," she says, and everyone laughs. "One at a time first."

It's beautiful, all that she says. I keep looking at Bubbles because it feels like the words could be about her and me, not all the specifics, but the feelings. Her and me have been through the dark too, and we've shared it. We've been there during each other's bad times. She helped me. I hope I helped her. We know it all, and we love each other. Not that we've said those words yet. But we do.

At the end of her vows, Amalphia holds one hand of each man and speaks to them both. "I love you. I always will. I don't know how to say it to show how big it is. I love your laughter. I love your eyes. I love your penises."

I laugh. But the main sound from the guests is like a hushed gasp, almost a sigh.

"I'm going to stop now," she says. "I'm overwhelmed, and I'm embarrassing people."

"Not us," said Aleks, stepping up onto the stone. "Every man likes to hear this." There's more applause before he goes on to tell a history of their relationship and Will joins them on the stone.

Amalphia puts the two men's hands together. They look at one another and the sun seems to grow brighter behind them, to burn with a greater fire. Yeah, I am a walking cliché at the moment. I smile at Bubbles through the 'I love you' vows, and she smiles back.

"And look what it has all led to," says Amalphia, sweeping her arm round in an action that takes in all of us: their children, their friends, Crispin Truelove, who has been unusually quiet today, and Holly, who's mopping her eyes with a tissue.

All three kiss. And kiss again. And again.

Justin approaches the stone and coughs. "It's getting embarrassing now," he says. "We all expect cake at some point, you know."

So Sun says the 'year and a day' thing.

Aleks shakes his head. "Forever."

"Forever," Will and Amalphia agree, and Sun ties their wrists together with three ribbons of white, silver and gold.

People start to move towards the newly married three, but Bubbles holds me back. "There's something I need to check," she says and pulls me down into a kiss.

We're kissing. Like we haven't done in half of forever. Not since that summer two years ago. But, now, it's like we never stopped. Why did we? Why would we? I could do this forever. But she pulls back. Oh no. What's happening?

She's walking to the now-vacant flat stone. She steps up on it. No one but me notices; everyone else is round the wedding party.

Bubbles laughs and holds out her hands to me. I'm drawn forward. I take her hands and step up to stand with her.

"Shall we?" she says.

I look at her. "Shall we...?"

"A year and a day," she says. "We could see how it goes. What d'you think? Alexander Zolotov, will you get handfasted with me?"

51

YOUR BEAUTY. IT'S WHAT I dwell on to keep me sane now. My perfect boy. I do not speak of your looks, though obviously you have your father's handsome appearance. I speak of your heart, your beautiful soul. Women will flock to you. Men too. But you need to seek out the one who sees your soul and loves you for that, the true you. Your soulmate. Your heart's match. One who truly values and cherishes you.

I pray – yes, I even do that now – that this will come to pass. I hope you find her, or him, beautiful Alexander. I wish you great happiness. A life in the light.

I love you,

Michelle Manteith

———ℓℓ———

I stare at the red and green ribbons that Sun found in her bag and used to bind our wrists together. There's so much more I want to say to Bubbles, Serena, than just our basic willingness to make this commitment and the quick vows we just said. We said 'I love you.' Important words. Never-said-before words. True words. And it feels like there's been no time to take them in, to take it all in. It's all happening so fast. This. Wonderful this. Us. My mind is fast too; it's racing ahead to: what now? Am I going to London with her? Is she staying here? Are we going to be long distance? Maybe I should get a job?

The thoughts fade as we're surrounded by people, well-wishers, family. Holly is saying: "Oh man." Crispin is asking if it's the greatest love story never told: 'ballet boy gone bad' falls for a beautiful mermaid. His huge voice echoes round the stones.

"Watch him," warns Amalphia, wiping her eyes with one of Holly's tissues. "He'll make it into a film. But you two! I'm so happy for you."

"I have to give it to you," says Justin. "That was an accomplished upstage."

"Oh, we didn't mean to do that!" says Bubbles. "It was a completely spur-of-the-moment thing."

"Really?" asks Will with a grin at me.

"Not the feelings," I say. But he knows that.

"But the feeling that this was what we should do," says Bubbles. "I just had to jump up on the stone and ask you."

"I know," I say because, despite my brain's run ahead, it all feels so right, and so true; the cliché's are lining up in this one.

"We will have to give you a wedding gift," says my father. "Maybe a holiday?"

"Time to talk about that later," says Amalphia. "I think Alexander and Serena need some time alone, and we've got a medieval feast to attend. Time for cake!" she calls to the guests, and they begin to wander away down the forest path, each one gifting a hug or kind words to Amalphia, Aleks and Will, and then Bubbles and me too.

Me and Bubbles. Bubbles and me. Married! Sort of. In a non-legal type of way. That she can run away from anytime she wants. Stop.

Simone hugs us, and it looks like there's tears in her eyes, but then she doesn't say anything about what just happened. She just tells us not to be too long as she's arranged all sorts of good things for us. "There's going to be feasting between the great hall walls, and then ballet and Shakespeare shorts in the theatre space. There's juggling, and dancing, and music. Everyone can see all the archaeology stuff too if they like; the centre is open just for this today."

I still don't know what to do about her, but I guess there's all the time in the world to decide.

There's hugs and surprise from Ariel, Jonasz, Henry and Clinton. They're happy. They're curious. But we'll talk later; everyone wants to talk later.

"Verily I say unto thee, we shall leave the young newlyweds in peace!" intones Crispin, and everyone obeys his command, and they all set off down the pine-tree path. "How about a nice little stay in Hollywood during the year and a day?" he suggests. "You could work together. You know Bevan and I have that historical planned. The two of you would be perfect!"

"Crispin!" says Amalphia.

"Going, going..." and he's gone.

And now we are six.

Us and my parents. And Justin. There's some complicated, ribbon-tangly hugging. Amalphia and Justin are both weepy. Amalphia holds his hand with her free hand.

"You two stay up here a while," she says to us. "The celebrations are on all day. Or go down to the house; make the most of it being empty. Sorry, am I being indelicate?"

"You mentioned penises in your vows," says Justin. "You sailed past indelicate then."

"True," admits Amalphia. "But we'll head to the castle now. I want to dance while we're still tied; it's fun. Oh, some people leave these ribbons on for days," she tells us, "but we abandon them once one of us goes to the bathroom. And, quite frankly, I don't want anything complicating my enjoyment of the giant chocolate cake Simone has promised me."

They start to walk towards the trees, but Amalphia suddenly turns about, pulling Will and Aleks in her wake.

"She would be really glad," she says to me. "Pleased for you both. I know it. Michelle," she adds unnecessarily.

"Come on, Malph, leave 'em be," says Will, circling her waist with his free arm.

We stand and watch them disappear into the dark path between the pines. Justin's voice carries back. "I'm quite overcome, Phi."

"We'll get you mead, or a tankard of ale..." is the beginning of Amalphia's reply, and then we're properly alone.

"They really should have tied him in too," I say. "He's a big part of that marriage."

We look at each other now. We smile. Soft. Noses together. And then she grabs the back of my head and we're kissing. Top lips. Bottom lips. I kiss her eyelids, and her ears. The ties are annoying; I want to hold her face and touch her hair without dragging her arm around.

She sits down on the grass and undoes the ribbons. I sit too. I take hold of her head, tip her chin up to me and kiss her again and again and again, and then just bury my face in her hair and it's so sweet, the sweetest thing. She is the sweetest, most joyful being on earth.

I sit back to look at her, to bask in her beauty and her love. I can feel it. I can see it in her eyes, beaming out at me. It returns to her in full; we have our own great big circle of love here, within this circle of stone.

Her blue eyes twinkle up at me as her fingertips trace all the parts of my face. "If everything else is as good as kissing you has always been, a year and a day might not be long enough."

I laugh at that. "Way to put pressure on a guy."

"No pressure. We don't have to if you don't want to. It could be a celibate year and day."

I love her naughtiness. I love her sparkle. I love Bubbles. Completely. I'm the one that's overwhelmed.

But not her, the instigator of this great event in our lives. She's calm and sensible today, with this, and that's good.

"What do you think about the film thing?" she says. "It could be fun. Working together. Acting. We liked it before."

"I don't know. I haven't thought about it. I'm having trouble thinking about anything but you."

"Who knew you were such a romantic, Alexander?"

"Only when it comes to you."

She tips her head back and fills the circle with laughter. "Let's take one thing at a time," she says, standing. "First we curtsey to the circle. That's right, isn't it? Amalphia sometimes does that when she leaves, I think? Like révérence at the end of class?"

She curtseys. I bow, properly low, with an ornate arm flourish that makes her laugh again.

"And now," she says. "We leave via the kissing gate. And from then on, everything will be magical."

And, as I tangle my fingers through hers and she pulls me along to the gate, I know that she's right. We're going to burn bright, the two of us, like stars rather than fire now. She looks round and smiles, and all is very, very well in the world.

Helpful Websites

- NHS page on getting help for drug addiction: https://www.nhs.uk/live-well/addiction-support/drug-addiction-getting-help/

- National Association for People Abused in Childhood: https://napac.org.uk/ Free (UK) Helpline 0808 801 0331

- The blog of Dr. Glenn Doyle, who specialises in trauma recovery: https://useyourdamnskills.com/

About the Author

AILISH SINCLAIR TRAINED AS a dancer and taught dance for many years, before working in schools to help children with special needs.

She lives in Scotland beside a loch with her husband and two children where she dances (medical conditions allowing) and writes and eats rather too much chocolate.

See the blog at ailishsinclair.com for posts about Scotland, castles, history, stone circles, dance, living with chronic illness, and writing.

More Ailish

Online

www.ailishsinclair.com

@AilishSinclair on X/Instagram/Threads

Contemporary Fiction:

A Dancer's Journey (series) (explicit content)

When dance student Amalphia Treadwell embarks on a secret relationship with her rich, handsome teacher, she has no idea of the danger that lurks in his new school in Scotland...

Titles: Tendu, Cabriole, Fouetté

Historical Fiction:

Sisters at the Edge of the World

From the misty hills of ancient Scotland emerges a tale of love, betrayal, and the fight for freedom. Set in the 1st century, the story includes the battle of Mons Graupius between the Romans and the Caledonian tribes. There's a neurodivergent main character and some rather complicated romance!

The Mermaid and the Bear

Set in a castle in Aberdeenshire (yes, the same castle), Ailish's debut novel blends an often overlooked period of history, the Scottish witchcraft accusations, in particular the 1597 Aberdeen witchcraft panic, with a love story.

Fireflies and Chocolate

Torn out of her isolated life in a Scottish castle, Elizabeth embarks on a determined quest to return home. Exhilarating adventures unfold on the high seas, love blossoms, and the chocolate, purchased in Benjamin Franklin's printing shop, is delicious!